Prescription for a Healthy Church

MINISTRY IDEAS TO NURTURE WHOLE PEOPLE

by

Jolene L. and Eugene C. Roehlkepartain

Group
Loveland, Colorado

Prescription for a Healthy Church: Ministry Ideas to Nurture Whole People

Copyright © 2000 Search Institute and Jolene L. Roehlkepartain

Visit our Web site: www.grouppublishing.com

Credits

Editor: Dave Thornton

Chief Creative Officer: Joani Schultz

Copy Editor: Janis Sampson

Art Director: Jeff Spencer

Designer/Computer Graphic Artist: Kristen Ellisor

Cover Art Director: Jeff A. Storm

Cover Designer: Coonts Design Group, LLC

Cover Photographer: Stock Illustration Source

Production Manager: Peggy Naylor

Roehlkepartain, Jolene L., 1962-
  Prescription for a healthy church : ministry ideas to nurture whole people / by Jolene L. and Eugene C. Roehlkepartain.
      p. cm.
  Includes bibliongraphical regerences.
  ISBN 0-7644-2215-4 (alk. paper)
   1. Christian education of children. 2. Church work with children. 3. Church work with youth. I. Roehlkepartain, Eugene C., 1962- II. Title

BV1475.2 R64 2000
259'.2--dc21

00-055150

10 9 8 7 6 5 4 3 2 1   09 08 07 06 05 04 03 02 01 00
Printed in the United States of America.

Dedication

To the people in the congregations who built our assets when we were growing up. Some of the people who went out of their way to bring out the best in Jolene while nurturing her skills, interests, and faith were Paul J. Christensen, Marty and Thelma Gavic, Rev. Merrill Gilbertson, Doug Howell, Gerri Jones, Don Martin, Rita Skone, and Randy Thompson. The asset builders for Gene included Glenn and Jeanine Boyd, Tom and Marilyn McMillan, Keith and Peggy Oliphant, Betty and Joe Hall, Joe Palmer, Ray and Ellen Deaver, Nan Brown, and Dr. Daniel Bagby. Thanks to you all.

Acknowledgments

This book builds on the efforts of many people and organizations. First and foremost, it relies on the knowledge gained through Search Institute's four-year project Uniting Congregations for Youth Development, of which Gene served as project director. This pilot initiative explored how to equip congregations of all faiths to build assets in youth within the congregation and in the broader community. Special thanks to the colleagues who were part of this project team and in other work with congregations: Ann Betz, Colette Illarde, James Conway, Rebecca Grothe, Jennifer Griffin-Wiesner, Ravinder Manku, and Peter C. Scales.

The project was supported through a generous grant from the DeWitt Wallace-Reader's Digest Fund, New York, New York. The fund's mission is to foster fundamental improvement in the quality of educational and career development opportunities for all school-age youth and to increase access to these improved services for young people in low-income communities. We appreciate the fund's vision in recognizing congregations as valued resources for today's young people.

This book also draws on Search Institute's efforts to encourage asset building in all sectors of communities across the United States. This initiative—which we call Healthy Communities • Healthy Youth—relies on the generous, long-term support of Lutheran Brotherhood, which supported the original research on developmental assets and has been an ongoing partner in asset building for the past decade. Lutheran Brotherhood is a member-owned organization of more than one million Lutherans joined together for financial security, outreach to church and community, and volunteer service. Lutheran Brotherhood demonstrates its stewardship through products and programs that serve Lutherans, strengthen communities, and aid Lutheran congregations and institutions.

It is also important to recognize those who laid the foundation for this book by developing the framework of developmental assets. First, thanks to Peter Benson, Search Institute's president, for giving birth to this idea and then empowering others to build upon and shape the idea. We also thank Nancy Leffert, who has been instrumental in conceptualizing the developmental assets for children from birth to age eleven.

This book might be very different if not for St. Luke Presbyterian Church, Minnetonka, Minnesota, where we were invited to try out ideas, experiment, and imagine possibilities for asset building. We particularly appreciate the encouragement and friendship of co-pastors Barbara Battin and Bill Chadwick.

Finally, we want to thank the creative team at Group Publishing for inviting us to write this book. Thanks to Thom Schultz, Joani Schultz, and Joel Fay, who initiated the early conversations that led to this book. Thanks to Dave Thornton, who proposed this project and worked with us to develop and edit the manuscript. It has been great to work with you again.

Table of Contents

Helping Children & Youth

GROW UP HEALTHY

Young people from four Lutheran Churches on Chicago's north side planned a joint worship service that included a human bingo game and a skit based on the New Testament parable of the ten wedding attendants. Not only did the worship service turn out well, but supportive adults found that the young people formed stronger ties to their respective congregations and strengthened their planning and decision-making skills.

* * *

A few years ago, less than ten adults at St. Joan of Arc Catholic Church in Columbus, Ohio, were involved in leading the youth program, which was growing rapidly. So Donna and Tom Berg, part-time ministry coordinators, began a program called It Takes a Whole Parish. Before long, 40 percent of the adults had expressed interest in helping. Consequently, many people in the congregation became regularly involved with young people.

* * *

Glendale Heights United Methodist Church in Durham, North Carolina, involves young people and adult congregation members in local service projects through an ongoing partnership with Oxford Manor, a local housing project. The partnership gives the young people of the church a chance to form intergenerational relationships and to make friends with young people with socioeconomic backgrounds different from their own.

* * *

In Riverside, California, more than thirty sixth-graders signed up for a seventeen-week program that included studying the Bible, doing homework, and memorizing Scripture passages. During the last week of the program, the children did a one-week service project. After the program, children were much more excited about the Bible and more responsible, and people within the church changed their view of young people, according to program leader Bill Russell of Victoria Community Church.

"We've discovered that kids will rise to the level you want them to as long as that level isn't unreasonable."[1]

* * *

When First Presbyterian Church of Crafton Heights in Pittsburgh, Pennsylvania, decided to rehabilitate and convert an old movie theater into a community recreation center, young people were involved in the whole process, says former youth worker Dave Carver. Young people sponsored a fund-raiser and helped with the renovation by hauling cement and busting down old walls. Altogether, they spent eighteen months on the project. "The kids most appreciated the fact that they could make a positive contribution," Carver remembers. "The church gave those kids the chance to do something right."

* * *

Six Sunday school children between the ages of six and twelve tend to the Prayer Line of the United Congregational Church of Keosauqua, Iowa. Church members leave their prayer requests on the Prayer Line's answering machine, and the children pray about the requests. The children see that they play an important role in helping others. They even see their own prayers answered from time to time. One woman sent a check to cover the cost of a pizza party that the children prayed to have but didn't have funding for!

* * *

What's going on with these congregations? Though they all have different activities and emphases, they also have something in common: They're all building "developmental assets." They're all providing for children and youth the positive building blocks that ensure that they will grow up healthy, caring, and responsible.

"Developmental assets" and "asset building" may not be familiar terms for talking about children, youth, and family ministry; but the terms represent a powerful, research-based approach that helps churches identify concrete, practical ways they can have a long-term impact in the lives of children and youth. The assets

guide them to make positive choices and avoid the problems and negative behaviors that are too widespread among young people throughout society.

Asset building doesn't replace a focus on helping young people grow in faith and discipleship; rather, it reinforces and shapes the "how" of nurturing faith. It also gives churches a concrete way to examine their ministries to ensure that they have the greatest impact in the real-world lives of children and youth.

What Young People Need to Grow Up Well

Asset building is not just another theory or program; it's a framework that grows out of extensive research by Minneapolis-based Search Institute on hundreds of thousands of young people across the United States. That research (along with research by many other scholars) focuses not on what's wrong with young people, but what's right—what makes a positive difference in kids' lives.

Search Institute researchers examined extensive research on kids to identify positive things that seemed to make a difference for young people. Then they used in-depth surveys to ask young people about those things.

The result was a set of developmental assets, essential building blocks for healthy development. The asset framework gives a clear picture of things that are important for helping children and teenagers avoid problems; overcome challenges; and make healthy, positive choices.

Researchers have grouped the forty assets into eight categories. The

AN ASSET-BUILDING CHURCH

Building Assets in Parents and Teenagers

At St. John of the Cross in Middlebury, Connecticut, the parish is intentional about building assets in young people and their parents. The parish creates service projects that teenagers and their parents can do together at different levels of involvement.

At the easiest level of involvement, parishioners drive other families to do volunteer work in a homeless shelter. For those who want more involvement, the parish offers a list of things that people in the shelter use, and families organize the collection of the items during Advent. At an even higher level of involvement, six families made the commitment of making a meal for the shelter once a month.

"There are different ways of getting involved that fit different families' needs and availability," says Thomas Bright, a member of the parish. "We try to make sure that this is a strong family focus so that families understand, learn, and grow with the young people."

An Attitude Check for Your Church

The statements on the left side of the page represent common attitudes that shape children, youth, and family ministries. The statements in the right column represent some of the key attitudes that contribute to building assets. Most churches are somewhere between the two statements. Where do you see your own church in each of these areas?

1. Focus on the negative, the problems, the fears

   Focus on the positives, the hopes, the possibilities

   | 1 | 2 | 3 | 4 | 5 |

2. Focus on programs

   Focus on relationships

   | 1 | 2 | 3 | 4 | 5 |

3. Age segregation

   Intergenerational relationships

   | 1 | 2 | 3 | 4 | 5 |

4. Short-term focus

   Long-term vision

   | 1 | 2 | 3 | 4 | 5 |

5. Unconnected activities without a clear purpose

   Activities connected to a vision of healthy development.

   | 1 | 2 | 3 | 4 | 5 |

6. Nurturing children and youth is the responsibility of program leaders and parents.

   Nurturing children and youth is the whole congregation's job.

   | 1 | 2 | 3 | 4 | 5 |

7. Youth as recipients

   Youth as leaders, contributors

   | 1 | 2 | 3 | 4 | 5 |

8. Families supporting the congregation's programming

   The congregation supporting and equipping families

   | 1 | 2 | 3 | 4 | 5 |

9. Isolation and competition

   Cooperation and support

   | 1 | 2 | 3 | 4 | 5 |

10. Commitment to "our kids"

    Commitment to "all kids"

    | 1 | 2 | 3 | 4 | 5 |

individual assets are explained in more detail in chapters 3-10. To get a sense of the entire framework, let's begin with the eight categories:

- **Support**—The first six assets highlight young people's need for support, care, and love in all areas of their lives. That support needs to begin in their families and extend to all their relationships. They also need to experience acceptance and care in the places they spend time, including their schools, neighborhoods, and churches. The support assets are explored more in depth in chapter 3.

- **Empowerment**—Young people need to be valued by their community and have opportunities to contribute to and serve others. For this to occur, they must feel safe. Search Institute has identified four empowerment assets (#7-#10), which are explained in chapter 4.

- **Boundaries and expectations**—Young people need to know what is expected of them and whether activities and behaviors are "in bounds" or "out of bounds." The expectations need to be modeled by responsible adults and peers. Boundaries and expectations (assets #11-#16) are examined in chapter 5.

- **Constructive use of time**—Young people need constructive, enriching opportunities for growth through activities and programs in which they learn skills, develop creativity and discipline, build relationships, and are guided by caring, responsible

adults. They also need to spend quality time at home. Chapter 6 focuses on the constructive use of time (assets #17-#20).

- **Commitment to learning**—Young people need to develop a lifelong commitment to education and learning. They need to be motivated, challenged, and stimulated to learn and grow. Commitment to learning (assets #21-#25) is explored more in depth in chapter 7.

- **Positive values**—Young people need to develop strong values that guide their choices. Positive values (assets #26-#31) are explained in chapter 8.

- **Social competencies**—Young people need skills and competencies that equip them to make positive choices, to build relationships, and to succeed in life. Chapter 9 examines social competencies (assets #32-#36).

- **Positive identity**—Young people need a strong sense of their own power, purpose, worth, and promise. A positive identity (assets #37-#40) is addressed in chapter 10.

The basic asset framework, which includes these eight categories, is the same for all children and teenagers. But we all know that what a baby needs is quite different from what a teenager needs. So Search Institute has shaped the assets to be appropriate for the major developmental phases during childhood and adolescence. Thus the forty assets are age-appropriate and equivalent (though may be worded

AN ASSET-BUILDING CHURCH

Empowering Young People

While a number of congregations build assets by empowering young people, they often do it through leadership and decision making about programming. At Kirkwood Baptist Church in St. Louis, Missouri, they also empower young people through leadership and decision making about budgets.

Cherie Smith, associate pastor for Christian education, makes sure that each teenager gets a copy of the church budget. In the budget, youth see how much of the offering is put into ministry for them. "One year when they found out that the choir tour cost $11,000 and their $150 fee only added up to about $5,000, they really understood how much the church gives them." She encourages young people to not only be the receivers but also contributors to the church.

"I have really discovered over my years working with youth that they will get the gospel better if they are doing the gospel," Smith says. Instead of just getting together to talk, the young people serve. The church's soup kitchen ministry was receiving socks from all over the country, and the soup kitchen director was feeling overwhelmed with all the sock sorting. Then the young people pitched in. For about four weeks, they sorted the socks while talking about school and their own lives.

The Impact of Developmental Assets

This table indicates the percentage of young people who report engaging in patterns of high-risk behaviors (such as using drugs and getting involved in sexual intercourse) and those who have positive behaviors and attitudes (such as helping others and succeeding in school), based on the number of assets Search Institute researchers found that young people reported having.

PATTERNS OF RISK-TAKING BEHAVIOR	0-10 Assets	11-20 Assets	21-30 Assets	31-40 Assets
Illicit drugs	42%	19%	6%	1%
Used illicit drugs three or more times in the past year.				
Sexual intercourse	33%	21%	10%	3%
Has had sexual intercourse three or more times in lifetime.				
Violence	61%	35%	16%	6%
Has engaged in three or more acts of fighting, hitting, injuring a person, carrying or using a weapon, or threatening physical harm in the past year.				
Depression/suicide	40%	25%	13%	4%
Is frequently depressed and/or has attempted suicide.				

POSITIVE BEHAVIORS AND ATTITUDES	0-10 Assets	11-20 Assets	21-30 Assets	31-40 Assets
Helps others	69%	83%	91%	96%
Helps friends or neighbors one or more hours per week.				
Succeeds in school	7%	19%	35%	53%
Gets mostly A's on report card.				
Values diversity	34%	53%	69%	87%
Places high importance on getting to know people of other racial/ethnic groups.				
Maintains good health	25%	46%	69%	88%
Pays attention to healthy nutrition and exercise.				

Based on survey data from 99,462 sixth- to twelfth-grade public school students in 213 towns and cities across the country.

differently) for each of five age groups:

- infants
(birth to twelve months);

- toddlers (thirteen to thirty-five months);

- preschoolers
(three to five years);

- elementary-age children
(six to eleven years); and

- teenagers (twelve to eighteen years), the focus of the original research.

The forty assets for each age group are listed on photocopiable handouts in the back of this book (pp. 133-143). You can distribute the copies to members of your church.

Assets Shape Young People's Lives

Often when people first read through the forty assets, they say: "What's the big deal? These are just common sense." There's truth in that response. There are no "secret ingredients" in the assets; they are just basic things young people need in their lives.

Yet these basic things are powerful building blocks of healthy development. Surveys of thousands of sixth- to twelfth-grade youth across the United States have found that the more assets young people experience, the more they engage in positive behaviors, such as volunteering and succeeding in school. The fewer assets they have, the more likely they are to engage in risk-taking behaviors, such as alcohol and other drug use, antisocial behavior, and violence. (See the "Impact of Developmental

AN ASSET-BUILDING CHURCH

Create a Ministry Around Young People

At the Netarts Friends Church in Tillamook, Oregon, youth director Matthew York Lacy pays close attention to each young person's gifts, interests, and talents. "If you see them taking an interest in service, then you do that. If you see them have some ability in acting, you do that," he says. "As facilitators for Christ, we should be working with the gifts that God has given."

Lacy also is aware that young people really like the Lazer Tag game, but his youth ministry isn't centered around Lazer Tag. "I'm not saying cater to the youth." Instead, he says, it's better to know the kids as individuals, to realize what they have to offer, and to understand what they're interested in rather than trying to plug them into an existing program that others think is good for them.

For example, the group went into Portland, Oregon, for its mission trip this year instead of going to Mexico. Some of the young people were upset because they were looking forward to having an adventure in another country. But Lacy discerned that some of the young people were being called to serve those in Portland. "It's all about having a positive relationship with Jesus so we can hear his leading so we know where we're supposed to be going." By blending a call to ministry with assets, churches can encourage young people to serve in meaningful ways.

AN ASSET-BUILDING CHURCH

Forming Asset-Building Partnerships

A number of churches have linked up to provide asset-building programming that they couldn't do alone.

• Three churches in Santa Clara County, California, launched a joint confirmation class based on the assets. It included parent education classes that focused on how parents can be partners in asset building.

• Union Congregational Church and Aldersgate Methodist Church in St. Louis Park, Minnesota, team up each summer to create a shared vacation Bible school for children.

• In Bridgeport, Connecticut, the Miracle Faith World Outreach and St. Joseph's of Stratford had a joint dance for their youth groups. The youth met beforehand to plan the specifics, including the games for the dance. A popular local DJ was booked to spin the music, and about one hundred young people signed up for the dance ahead of time.

Assets" table on page 12.)

Take the issue of violence, for example. Among young people who report having ten or fewer assets, 61 percent report being involved in patterns of violent activities (which were defined as three or more acts of serious violence in the past year). But among those reporting thirty-one or more of the forty assets, only 6 percent engaged in patterns of violence. This same pattern holds true for at least ten different areas of high-risk behavior including alcohol, tobacco, and other drug use; sexual activity; depression and attempted suicide; violence and other antisocial behavior; school problems; driving and alcohol; and gambling.

The opposite pattern occurs when we focus on positive attitudes and behaviors, such as affirmation of diversity. Among young people with thirty-one or more of the forty assets, 87 percent value getting to know people who are different from them. Yet only thirty-four percent of those with ten or fewer assets express this positive attitude.

In addition to the assets' power to protect young people from negative behaviors and promote positive behaviors, the assets also help young people bounce back from adversity or trauma, such as sexual abuse, alcoholism in the family, divorce, neglect, and poverty. Several prominent researchers in the field of resiliency have identified factors that make it more likely for young people to beat the odds.[2]

What Research Reveals About Assets

In virtually every community Search Institute has studied across the United States, the average young person (grades six to twelve) experiences only about half of the assets. In Search Institute studies of 213 communities, the average young person has only eighteen of the forty developmental assets.

In the ideal, Search Institute researchers suggest that a community should strive to ensure that all young people develop thirty or more of the forty assets. However, only 8 percent of young people have thirty-one or more of the forty assets. Thus the foundation for positive development is incomplete or fragile for 92 percent of middle and high school youth. This reality is true for all types of young people, both male and female, all grades surveyed, and from all racial/ethnic groups.

Research tells us three things about assets. First, the assets are powerful influences on young people's choices. They do not eliminate problems, but they could significantly reduce problems and increase positive behaviors among children and youth if more young people experienced more assets.

Second, the assets add up. While each asset is important and must be singularly understood, the most powerful message of developmental assets comes in seeing them as an entire, connecting framework. These assets have a cumulative effect—the more the better.

Third, these same forty assets have a positive impact in many areas of young people's lives, not just in one or two. Research shows that most of the assets affect many areas of young people's lives. For example, "other adult relationships" (asset #3) has been linked to reduced violence, substance abuse, anxiety, depression, and loneliness; and also to higher self-esteem, hope for the future, cheerfulness, and success in school. A similar list could be created for each of the forty assets.[3]

Thus, instead of always feeling fragmented by pressure to constantly shift direction to address whatever problem or crisis is currently in the headlines, asset building offers a consistent strategy for addressing many life issues and challenges. It's not a way of avoiding the problems; rather it gives young people the strengths they need to face the many challenges and opportunities they face, both now and in the future.

NOTES

1. Bill Russell, "Kids Quest," Children's Ministry Magazine (July/August 1998), 51-52.

2. See, for example, Emmy Werner and Ruth S. Smith, *Overcoming the Odds: High-Risk Children From Birth to Adulthood* (Ithaca: Cornell University Press, 1992).

3. See Peter C. Scales and Nancy Leffert, *Developmental Assets: A Synthesis of the Scientific Research on Adolescent Development* (Minneapolis: Search Institute, 1999).

Examining Assets

AMONG RELIGIOUS YOUNG PEOPLE

The research on youth in public schools clearly shows disturbingly low levels of assets for the vast majority of youth in this country. But what about the young people that are involved in church? Aren't they in better shape?

When we look at young people who are religiously active (spending at least an hour a week in religious programs, activities, or services), we do find that teenagers who are involved in a religious institution are more likely to report having developmental assets. On average, religious youth report having twenty of the forty assets, compared to fifteen assets among youth who are inactive or nonreligious.

In fact, religiously active youth are more likely than nonreligious or inactive youth to experience all but one of the forty assets (the exception being asset #10: safety). (The "Youth Who Report Experiencing Each Developmental Asset" chart (pp. 18-19) shows the difference between active and inactive/nonreligious youth on each of the forty assets.)

Excluding asset #19: religious community (which was used to measure activity levels), the four greatest differences are all clearly related to congregational involvement:

- asset #9: service to others (a 24 percent difference between active and inactive youth),

- asset #15: positive peer influence (a 20 percent difference),

- asset #18: youth programs (a 24 percent difference), and

- asset #31: restraint (a 25 percent difference).

This research could be interpreted as saying that churches don't need to worry about building assets, since young people who come to church already have more assets. Yet only 11 percent of religious youth experience thirty-one or more of the assets, and 11 percent of religious

youth experience ten or fewer of the assets. In addition, only sixteen of the forty assets are experienced by a majority (50 percent or more) of religious youth. Or, put another way, twenty-four of the assets are experienced by fewer than half of the young people who regularly attend churches and other religious institutions.

These findings suggest that there is still much work to be done to build assets among young people in churches. In addition, churches could be a great resource for youth in communities if they would actively reach and serve community youth.

Connecting Asset Building With Faith and Ministry

If assets were simply good things for kids, some churches would probably say, "That's great for public schools or after-school programs, but what does it have to do with the church? After all, we're in the faith business." To be sure, Search Institute intentionally developed the asset framework to be relevant and accepted by many different institutions and perspectives within U.S. society. Yet there are also important, deep connections between asset building and the specific mission and mandate of the Christian church. Let's look at a few of these connections.

Lifestyle connections—Ted Melnyk is director of Project 40 for the Pittsburgh Leadership Network in Pittsburgh, Pennsylvania. Project 40 is an intensive, creative project to integrate assets into Pittsburgh churches. However, Melnyk says he has received resistance from churches when he talks about the framework of developmental assets. "It's not Christian," they maintain. "Why would we use it in our church?"

To respond to these concerns, Melnyk developed a series of forty youth Bible studies—one on each asset. "After researching and trying to create a scripturally based curriculum for each of these assets," he says, "I believe we in the church have much to learn from this research as we minister to young people." He says the broad range of issues in the asset framework acts as a reminder of real-world issues in kids' lives that the church needs to, but often doesn't, address.

One of the characteristics of effective children's and youth ministry is that it meets kids in their world, addressing real-world issues and concerns through the perspective of faith and Scripture.

And that's what the assets present: a fresh way—a positive and research-based perspective—to look at the real-life issues that children and youth face daily.

There's nothing new about the church addressing important life issues. How many churches already address issues of alcohol and other drugs, sexuality, music, dating, school, family issues, and other topics? What the assets offer is a different, positive way to look at kids' lives.

Scripture connections—One way to look at the connections between asset building and the church is to identify Scripture passages that tie to each asset. And, in fact, there are natural connections between each developmental asset and selected Bible passages. The "Connecting Assets to Scripture" chart suggests one or more Old and New Testament references for each of the forty developmental assets. (Consider using these references as a starting point for sermons or Bible studies on assets.)

Faith connections—Finally, building assets also builds faith. While Search Institute has only preliminary research to support this assertion, there are at least two reasons to believe it's true:

1. Young people with more assets are also more likely to place a priority on religious involvement and spirituality. Search Institute research has found that the more assets young people experience, the more likely they are to say that faith and spirituality are important to them. And young people with more assets are also more likely to be active in their congregation. The "Stats about Faith and Assets" box shows these connections, based on Search Institute research on almost one hundred thousand sixth- to twelfth-grade youth.

It's important to note that this kind of research doesn't show what causes what. It could be that young people with more assets are more open to or ready for spirituality and faith. Or it may be that congregational involvement, spiritual practices, and a faith commitment lead to more assets. In reality, it's

AN ASSET-BUILDING CHURCH

An Important Outreach

Several years ago First Baptist Church of Los Angeles made a major commitment to serve young people in its neighborhood through a recreation and arts center. The congregation wanted to give young people a safe place and constructive way to spend their time.

Despite good intentions, programs, and supervision, the center itself became a gang hangout. "We had hoped to build an accepting environment of safety," youth worker Jim Hopkins said. "But they saw it as just another safe place to continue gang and drug activities." So the center had to close down.

Rather than giving up on what it saw as an important outreach, the congregation looked to partnerships in the community to meet the needs. It began working with the YMCA to develop a more structured and controlled program that would include more values education and drug education. Although the new program didn't reach as many youth, it had a much greater impact on those involved.

Youth Who Report Experiencing

This list shows the percentage of young people that have each of the forty developmental assets, based on Search Institute survey data from 99,462 sixth- to twelfth-grade public school students in 213 towns and cities across the country. It also shows the percentages of religiously active youth* and inactive or nonreligious youth who report having each asset.

ASSET	TOTAL SAMPLE	RELIGIOUSLY ACTIVE YOUTH	INACTIVE/NON-RELIGIOUS YOUTH
Support			
#1: Family support	64%	69%	55%
#2: Positive family communication	26%	30%	19%
#3: Other adult relationships	41%	46%	31%
#4: Caring neighborhood	40%	46%	29%
#5: Caring school climate	24%	28%	17%
#6: Parental involvement in schooling	29%	34%	21%
Empowerment			
#7: Community values youth	20%	24%	13%
#8: Youth as resources	24%	29%	16%
#9: Service to others	50%	58%	34%
#10: Safety	55%	53%	58%
Boundaries and Expectations			
#11: Family boundaries	43%	48%	33%
#12: School boundaries	46%	49%	40%
#13: Neighborhood boundaries	46%	50%	39%
#14: Adult role models	27%	32%	17%
#15: Positive peer influence	60%	67%	47%
#16: High expectations	41%	44%	33%
Constructive Use of Time			
#17: Creative activities	19%	22%	13%
#18: Youth programs	59%	67%	43%
#19: Religious community**	64%	–	–
#20: Time at home	50%	53%	44%

Each Developmental Asset

ASSET	TOTAL SAMPLE	RELIGIOUSLY ACTIVE YOUTH	INACTIVE/NON-RELIGIOUS YOUTH
Commitment to Learning			
#21: Achievement motivation	63%	69%	53%
#22: School engagement	64%	68%	55%
#23: Homework	45%	49%	38%
#24: Bonding to school	51%	57%	40%
#25: Reading for pleasure	24%	27%	20%
Positive Values			
#26: Caring	43%	48%	34%
#27: Equality and social justice	45%	49%	38%
#28: Integrity	63%	66%	58%
#29: Honesty	63%	67%	55%
#30: Responsibility	60%	64%	54%
#31: Restraint	42%	51%	26%
Social Competencies			
#32: Planning and decision making	29%	32%	22%
#33: Interpersonal competence	43%	48%	36%
#34: Cultural competence	35%	37%	31%
#35: Resistance skills	37%	42%	28%
#36: Peaceful conflict resolution	44%	50%	32%
Positive Identity			
#37: Personal power	45%	48%	39%
#38: Self-esteem	47%	49%	42%
#39: Sense of purpose	55%	58%	48%
#40: Positive view of personal future	70%	74%	63%

*"Religiously active youth" are those who report spending at least an hour each week "going to programs, groups, or services at a church, synagogue, mosque, or other religious or spiritual place."

**This asset is the basis for distinguishing between religious and nonreligious/inactive youth.

Based on survey data from 99,462 sixth- to twelfth-grade public school students in 213 towns and cities across the country.

Connecting Assets to Scripture

You can use Scripture to emphasize the importance of each of the forty developmental assets. Here are Old and New Testament passages that relate to each asset.

ASSET	OLD TESTAMENT	NEW TESTAMENT
#1: Family support	Deuteronomy 6:1-9	1 Timothy 3:2-4
#2: Positive family communication	Proverbs 15:1-4	Ephesians 4:15-16; 6:4
#3: Other adult relationships	2 Kings 2	2 Timothy 1:1-14
#4: Caring neighborhood	Leviticus 19:18, 33-34	Mark 12:31-33
#5: Caring school climate	Ezekiel 34:11-15	Mark 9:37
#6: Parent involvement in schooling	Proverbs 22:6	Luke 2:41-52
#7: Community values children and youth	Jeremiah 1:5-8	Matthew 19:13-15
#8: Youth as resources	1 Samuel 16	1 Timothy 4:12
#9: Service to others	Genesis 41:41-43	Romans 12:9-13
#10: Safety	Psalm 12:6-8	1 Peter 1:3-7
#11: Family boundaries	Exodus 20:12; Proverbs 29:17	Hebrews 12:5-13 Ephesians 6:1-4
#12: School boundaries	Psalm 7:7-8	Titus 3:1-2
#13: Neighborhood boundaries	Leviticus 19:15-18	Ephesians 4:25-28
#14: Adult role models	1 Samuel 3	Hebrews 11; 13:7
#15: Positive peer influence	1 Samuel 20	Philemon 17
#16: High expectations	Exodus 3–4	2 Thessalonians 3:6-13
#17: Creative activities	Psalms 148–150	Ephesians 5:19-20
#18: Youth programs	Ecclesiastes 3:1-8	Acts 17:22-34
#19: Religious community	Isaiah 35	Romans 12:4-8
#20: Time at home	Ruth 1:16-18	Luke 15:11-32
#21: Achievement motivation	Nehemiah 2:11-18	Hebrews 12:1-2
#22: School engagement	Exodus 31:1-5	Colossians 3:23-24
#23: Homework	Ezra 7:8-10	John 7:14-16
#24: Bonding to school	Psalm 27:11	Romans 13:1-3
#25: Reading for pleasure	Jeremiah 36:1-10	Acts 15:22-35
#26: Caring	2 Kings 5:1-3, 7-15	Luke 10:25-37
#27: Equality and social justice	Amos 5:24	Matthew 25:34-36
#28: Integrity	Micah 6:8	2 Thessalonians 2:13-17
#29: Honesty	Proverbs 16:13; 24:26	Luke 3:12-13
#30: Responsibility	Ezekiel 18:1-9	Luke 16:1-13
#31: Restraint	Numbers 25:1-5	1 Thessalonians 4:3
#32: Planning and decision making	Isaiah 1:1-5	Luke 14:28-33
#33: Interpersonal skills	Proverbs 18:16	1 Timothy 6:18
#34: Cultural competence	Isaiah 11:1-10	Romans 15:4-13
#35: Resistance skills	Proverbs 28:4-5	1 Corinthians 10:13
#36: Peaceful conflict resolution	Isaiah 2:1-5	Matthew 5:9
#37: Personal power	1 Kings 17:7-16	Romans 12:1-8
#38: Self-esteem	Psalm 139:13	John 8:31-36
#39: Sense of purpose	Isaiah 43:1-7	2 Timothy 4:5-11
#40: Positive view of personal future	Jeremiah 29:11-12	Luke 6:20-31

probably a combination of the two. In either case, both high assets and high spirituality and religious involvement work together to have a positive impact in young people's lives.

2. Research shows that many of the same things that are important for nurturing faith are also important for building assets. For example, Search Institute conducted a study of youth and adults in The Lutheran Church-Missouri Synod and identified thirty qualities of congregational life that nurture a strong, mature faith.[1] Of those thirty qualities, twenty-two tie directly to one of the eight categories of assets. (See the "Church Qualities That Build Faith and Assets" box.) Thus the very things that build assets also help to nurture a Christian faith.

Ministry connections—Many things that are basic elements of effective ministry with children, youth, and families are strategies that tie directly to asset building. The assets framework offers a new perspective and focus for many of the goals and priorities that churches already have for their ministries.

Search Institute surveyed five hundred religious youth workers in seven communities, asking them about how important various strategies are for their work with youth. The "How Developmental Assets Connect to Ministry Priorities" box shows the percentages of youth workers who say each goal is important and how many say they achieve that goal "very well." Then it shows how that strategy ties directly to one or more of the forty developmental assets.

AN ASSET-BUILDING CHURCH

Offering Challenging Choices

When the youth group showed up at Ankeny Presbyterian Church in Ankeny, Iowa, they were expecting to order pizza. That's what they always did, and each teenager usually brought three dollars. But Mary Kohlsdorf, the youth director, gave the group two choices: either order pizza like they did every time or pool all their money to fix something cheap and use all the leftover money to buy something for the homeless shelter.

"For a minute they just kind of looked at me and said 'you're kidding me,'" she says. But then someone suggested that the group make macaroni and cheese since three dollars could probably feed the entire group. So the group divided up. One group went to the grocery store to buy macaroni and cheese to cook, and the other went to a Wal-Mart store and bought towels, shampoo, soap, and other necessities for the homeless shelter in the community.

"Here was a time we were gathering to eat—but instead of stuffing our faces, which we can do—we pooled our resources to help somebody else," Kohlsdorf says.

Church Qualities That Build Faith & Assets

A Search Institute study of youth and adults in The Lutheran Church-Missouri Synod identified thirty qualities of congregational life that help people grow in faith. Twenty-two of those qualities also connect to one of the eight categories of developmental assets. Percentages represent youth surveyed in The Lutheran Church-Missouri Synod who report this quality in their congregation.

For more information on this study, see Eugene C. Roehlkepartain, Margaret Hinchey, I. Shelby Andress, and Jennifer Griffin-Wiesner, *Strategic Youth Ministry* (Loveland, CO: Group, 2000).

Permission to photocopy this page granted for local church use. Copyright © Search Institute and Jolene L. Roehlkepartain. Published in *Prescription for a Healthy Church: Ministry Ideas to Nurture Whole People* by Group Publishing, Inc., P.O. Box 481, Loveland, CO 80539.

SUPPORT

The congregation has a warm, welcoming, and friendly climate.	52%
Adults and children spend quality time together.	35%
People feel that others in the congregation care about them.	63%
People take time to get to know each other.	42%
The congregation helps members meet their personal needs.	35%
Youth often experience care and support from an adult.	27%
The congregation intentionally strengthens family life.	44%

EMPOWERMENT

The congregation involves youth in decision making.	19%
The congregation makes use of members' talents.	46%
The congregation involves many people in decision making.	36%
Many members share responsibility for the congregation's ministry.	36%

CONSTRUCTIVE USE OF TIME

People spend three or more hours per month in Christian education.	62%
People get a lot out of worship.	58%

COMMITMENT TO LEARNING

The congregation has a thinking climate that encourages questions and expects learning.	23%
The congregation has quality youth education.	43%
Christian education for all ages emphasizes interactive learning.	18%

POSITIVE VALUES

The congregation shows love and concern for people in the community.	19%
The congregation helps members apply faith to daily life.	44%

SOCIAL COMPETENCIES

The congregation experience little conflict.	52%
The congregation teaches people how to share their faith with others.	41%
The congregation deals well with conflict.	35%

POSITIVE IDENTITY

The congregation has a clear vision.	50%

Outreach connections—One of the challenges churches face today is that they are often viewed with suspicion by others in the community. That suspicion is heightened when people from the church use religious language to talk about what they do for kids.

The asset-building approach can build bridges into the community. It gives churches a positive language to talk about what they can offer young people. It begins to open doors for the church to touch the lives of young people in the community. It makes it possible for churches to build or renew respect and trust in the community.

In short, having more assets gives children and youth the kinds of strength, guidance, and support they need to make responsible, faithful choices. Assets also help the church's ministry stay grounded in the realities and needs of young people and their families. And the assets provide a language and framework that help people open up to the contributions that churches can make in their communities on behalf of children, youth, and families.

None of these reasons imply that asset building should replace a specific focus on nurturing faith, teaching Scripture, and helping young people become committed disciples of Jesus Christ. Those tasks remain essential to the mission and ministry of the church. But asset building can strengthen and focus ministry, tying it to the real-world issues and needs of today's children, youth, and families. And assets offer concrete ways to build healthy relationships.

Stats About Faith and Assets

Search Institute surveys of one hundred thousand sixth- to twelfth-grade youth in 213 communities across the United States have found that the more assets young people have, the more likely they are to believe being religious or spiritual is important and to attend religious activities each week.

	If 1-10 assets	If 11-20 assets	If 21-30 assets	If 31-40 assets
Believe being religious or spiritual is "quite" or "extremely" important.	26%	47%	67%	81%
Spend an hour or more each week in religious programs, groups, or worship services.	38%	62%	79%	90%

Based on survey data from 99,462 sixth- to twelfth-grade public school students in 213 towns and cities across the country.

AN ASSET-BUILDING CHURCH

Teaching and Acting

Youth director Alan Ramsey believes that young people need a commitment to learning while acting on their desire to serve others. At the Fellowship Evangelical Free Church in Knoxville, Tennessee, Ramsey requires that young people go through four training sessions each time they go on a weeklong service or mission project.

Last year Ramsey emphasized the theme of "Reaching Out to Others" and connected Scriptures to the mission project. Each night during the trip, young people talked about what happened during the day and discussed reflective questions. Senior high students journaled as part of their learning. All this homework prepared them for their return to the church. That's when young people shared their experiences with parents, sponsors, and other young people at a missions night.

Hundreds of Ways to Build Assets

The framework of developmental assets isn't a program or a specific ministry strategy. Rather, it's a perspective and focus that you can bring to all areas of ministry and congregational life. It can affect how you relate to children and youth. It can shape where you try to involve young people throughout the church. It can challenge you to try new ideas for strengthening your programs and activities that reach children, youth, and families.

For example, the Lutheran Church of the Reformation in St. Louis Park, Minnesota, has adopted asset building as a focal point for its ministry. In fact, asset building became a focus for a year-long emphasis during worship. The pastor, Dennis Ormseth, identified Scriptures that fit with particular assets. Worship services included sermons, lay readings, and skits on asset building.

"Since we started talking about assets here, members of the congregation will show up at the Sunday morning coffee hour and pick up children they see in the room, give them hugs, and talk and laugh with them," Ormseth says.[2]

The church also created a free baby-sitting program called Kids Night Out. This program allows parents to have free child care so they can do what they need or enjoy some recreation, while feeling confident that their children are being well cared for by members of the church. Pastor Ormseth also has been a key leader in running Children First, the asset-building initiative for the entire community of

St. Louis Park.

Each of the next eight chapters focuses on one of the eight categories of developmental assets. We introduce the asset and how it fits with the church, and show how many young people report having the asset, based on Search Institute's surveys of almost one hundred thousand sixth- to twelfth-grade students in public schools in twenty-three states during the 1996-97 school year. (In cases where a particular asset is worded for another part of the community, we show how it also applies to the church.) Then we give dozens of ideas for how you can build that asset in the following areas:

- church nurseries
- children's ministry
- youth ministry
- family ministry
- Christian education
- intergenerational ministry
- community outreach

In addition, we offer tips and work sheets to help you build the assets. We also introduce you to many churches around the country that are building assets in creative and inspiring ways.

How Developmental Assets Connect

A Search Institute survey of five hundred religious youth workers found that most of them share youth development goals, but they are dissatisfied with their ability to achieve these goals. This chart shows the connections of many of these top goals of youth workers to Search Institute's framework of forty developmental assets.

Youth Workers' Goal	Goal Is Very Important	Achieve Goal Very Well	Asset Connections
Helping young people apply faith to daily decisions	88%	25%	#32: Planning and decision making
Nurturing a lifelong commitment	88%	22%	#39: Sense of purpose
Providing a safe and caring place for young people	84%	64%	#10: Safety #5: Caring school climate
Developing young people's skills and values	81%	24%	#26-#31: Positive values #32-#36: Competencies
Keeping young people involved in the congregation	78%	21%	#19: Religious community
Building caring relationships with other young people	77%	30%	#15: Positive peer influence
Encouraging self-respect and dignity	76%	35%	#37-#40: Positive identity
Providing positive activities to help young people avoid negative behaviors	69%	43%	#18: Youth programs #19: Religious community
Reaching out to serve young people at risk	68%	9%	#1-#40: All the assets
Helping young people build caring relation-ships with adults	65%	25%	#3: Other adult relationships
Nurturing a commitment to service in young people	64%	22%	#9: Service to others #26: Caring

Getting Started With a Positive Perspective

The implications of asset building for congregations are deep and long-term. They can touch virtually every area of church life. Every time we talk to a group about asset building, someone comes up with a new way the assets can be applied. That's what's so fun—and challenging—about asset building! You start to see it informing everything you do.

So it may take years before you're ready to say that your church is an "asset-building church." But the journey begins with becoming intentional about the positive focus on children and youth, emphasizing the need to build strengths. How can your church begin to promote a positive, asset-building vision?

- Cultivate positive attitudes toward children and youth in the congregation. Educate congregational leaders and members about the positive things they can expect from young people.

- Give adults a chance to get to know children and teenagers. Negative stereotypes can fade as people actually get to know each other.

- Provide opportunities for children and youth to contribute to the congregation through leadership and service. Publicly affirm and celebrate young people's contributions.

- Focus on nurturing relationships between young people and adults as much as you encourage relationships to build between young people.

- Be clear about boundaries and expectations with young people. Leaders unwittingly feed negative images when they don't insist that children and teenagers act with appropriate boundaries in the congregation. People have a right to be upset with young people if they damage property in the congregation or do not respect the rights of others.

- Challenge negative stereotypes of children and youth.

Keep in mind that a positive vision does not mean closing your eyes to the negatives. Nor does it imply a Pollyannaish "don't worry, be happy" attitude. Young people do face difficult, sometimes tragic problems. And some young people get into serious trouble. These issues must be addressed. But the way you deal with them will be profoundly different from an asset-building perspective.

Asset building opens new vistas to explore and new skills to build that will increase their effectiveness in serving children and youth. This exploration by a congregation can renew energy and commitment to young people and raise awareness of and respect for the role that people in children, youth, and family ministry have in the life of the *entire* congregation.

NOTES

1. See Eugene C. Roehlkepartain, Margaret Hinchey, I. Shelby Andress, and Jennifer Griffin-Wiesner, *Strategic Youth Ministry* (Loveland, CO: Group, 2000).

2. Michael L. Sherer, "Building Servants," The Lutheran 11, no. 2 (February 1998): 14-16.

CHAPTER 2

-27-

Supporting Children & Youth

Support is an essential ingredient that kids need to grow up healthy and faithful. Researchers consistently find that support makes a huge difference in the health and well-being of people of all ages—infants, children, teenagers, and adults. Many researchers believe that a caring and supportive relationship with an adult is the most critical factor in helping young people grow up healthy.

In addition, feeling supported and cared for are important faith-nurturing ingredients in children and youth. For example, a Search Institute study of more than three thousand youth in six major denominations found that being part of a "warm" and "caring" church helped young people grow in their faith.[1] Another Search Institute study in The Lutheran Church-Missouri Synod found that many support-related experiences in church strengthened young people's faith:

● Adults and children spend quality time together at church.

● Youth feel others in the congregation care about them.

● People take time to get to know each other.

● The congregation intentionally strengthens family life.

● Young people often experience care and support from an adult.[2]

The support assets particularly highlight the need for positive inter-generational relationships outside the immediate family (asset #3). Adults can nurture informal relationships with children and youth in their neighborhood (asset #4), in the congregation, and at work. Everywhere young people go, they need to feel welcomed, valued, and supported.

Congregations have the potential to increase young people's experiences of support in all three areas: family, intergenerational relationships, and caring institutions. For families with teenagers, it may mean educating parents about new ways to show support to teenagers who no longer respond to the ways they were supported when they were younger. For families with young children, it may mean giving families meaningful service opportunities that they can do together that has age-appropriate tasks for the children. Members of the congregation represent an often untapped source of intergenera-tional relationships, both formal and informal. Finally, congregations can examine their own culture to discover whether young people feel welcomed and cared for when they participate.

ASSET #1:

Family Support

Consistent love, comfort, encouragement, and support are essential for children and teenagers to grow up healthy. Each family demonstrates its caring in its own way, but researchers have shown that the care must be positive, consistent, and responsive. Congregations can encourage families to support their children by offering educational opportunities for parents to learn more ways to be supportive and by creating programs that promote family togetherness rather than sending members of the family off in different directions.

A key to family support is parents responding appropriately to the child's needs. Researchers Silvia Bell and Mary Ainsworth found that parents who answered their infants' cries immediately and consistently during the first few months of life had infants who cried less frequently and for shorter amounts of time.[3] As children grow older, the kinds of support they need changes, but the need doesn't go away. Even as they become more independent, teenagers need to know their parents will be there for them.

For children and teenagers of all ages, researchers have classified "supportive parents" as ones who are nurturing, close, intimate, and who do not use harsh punishment to set and enforce boundaries. However, the judges of these attributes are the children and teenagers, not the adults.[4] It's the young people's perceptions that indicate whether or not a family is supportive.

Unfortunately, Search Institute research reveals that young people are less likely to see their families as supportive as they go through the teenage years. While 79 percent of sixth-graders say their families are supportive, only 60 percent of twelfth-graders do. Overall, 64 percent of all young people report having the asset of family support. Sixty-five percent of all girls do, and 64 percent of all guys do.

ASSET #2:

Positive Family Communication

Family members communicate daily—from the first grunts in the morning to the good night wishes. While it's true that families are busy and in-depth conversations may be rare, all of the ways family members communicate with each other can give some important clues about how supportive a family is. The way family members look at each other during conversations, the way they talk to each other, and the words they choose greatly impact each child and teenager.

Congregations can nurture positive family communication by creating family events that encourage family members to talk to each other and start discussions on topics that they may not have talked about. Congregations also can teach parents loving ways to affirm and correct a young person so that a young person feels connected to the family while also receiving guidance.

Only 26 percent of all young people say they experience asset #2: positive family communication. Twenty-eight percent of all girls report having this asset compared to 24 percent of all guys. What's alarming, however, is that only 17 percent of twelfth-grade guys report having this asset. The twelfth-grade girls aren't in much better shape, with only 20 percent having this asset.

There is clearly a great opportunity for churches to help strengthen positive family communication asset. However, many youth don't see their churches helping much in this area.

The Support Assets

Asset #1: Family support — 64%

Asset #2: Positive family communication — 26%

Asset #3: Other adult relationships — 41%

Asset #4: Caring neighborhood — 40%

Asset #5: Caring school climate — 24%

Asset #6: Parent involvement in schooling — 29%

AN ASSET-BUILDING CHURCH

All Kinds of Support

They need parental support. They need the church support. They need the group support," says Rev. Mary E. Nesbit, pastor of the Greater St. James Fire Baptized Holiness Church in Detroit, Michigan. She's familiar with the different types of support that children and youth need. "Once you start working with them, listen to them. Hear them. Then use their ideas, even if sometimes you have to modify some of them. But let them have some input into what is going on."

A Search Institute study of 3,100 mainline Protestant youth found that only 31 percent of these young people believed their church was doing a good or excellent job helping them learn how to "talk better" with their parents.[5]

ASSET #3:

Other Adult Relationships

Children and teenagers need relationships with adults outside of their family: Sunday school teachers, youth workers, children's ministry workers, ministers, nursery volunteers, and members of the congregation at large. Researchers found that young people who had the highest self-worth, most positive hopes for the future, and most cheerfulness were young people who had social support from "special adults." These special adults can include anyone, such as a neighbor, a teacher, or an interested adult in the congregation.[6]

Congregations have a vital role in nurturing this asset. In fact, congregations are often seen as one of the last institutions where children and teenagers have access to other adults on a consistent basis. By promoting intergenerational events that encourage intergenerational relationships to form, children and teenagers can greatly benefit.

While 41 percent of all young people surveyed by Search Institute report having this asset, 43 percent of all girls compared to 39 percent of all guys say they experience other adult relationships. In fact, this is the only asset of the six support assets that actually goes up through the middle and high school years.

While 41 percent of sixth graders say they have this asset, 46 percent of twelfth-graders report having other adult relationships.

ASSET #4:

Caring Neighborhood

Children and teenagers feel less lonely when they feel a sense of neighborhood support.[7] Having neighbors to count on makes a big difference in the lives of young people. Neighbors who know young people's names and who go out of their way to greet and talk with young children give young people the sense that they are cared for.

Many congregations reach out to the neighborhood in which they're located to build this sense of community and caring. They expand their ministry past the church building and into the neighborhood.

Another way churches can help to build the caring neighborhood asset is to help all members recognize the ways they can show care in their own neighborhoods as part of their "lay ministry" in their community. By encouraging members to show Christian love with children on their block or in their apartment building (and in other places where they see kids), churches help members live their faith all week.

Forty percent of all young people reporting having asset #4: caring neighborhood. Girls (41 percent) are more apt to say they have this asset than guys (38 percent), and a higher percentage of sixth-graders have this asset than twelfth-graders.

CHAPTER 3

ASSET #5:

Caring School Climate

The people with whom young people come into contact each day impacts a school's climate. That includes the way the bus driver treats a child or a teenager. It also involves other students, teachers, counselors, coaches, cooks, custodians, school secretaries, volunteers—even the principal. One elementary school principal started each school day by standing at the entrance of the school; there he greeted each student and called them each by name. That's one way to create a caring school climate.

For young children, these climates include child-care centers, preschools, church nurseries, Sunday school classes—essentially any type of out-of-home experience. What's key in creating a caring climate is the way the adults interact with children. And typically the one who has the most influence is a teacher. A caring teacher is one who has high expectations for students, is fair in dealing with a variety of students, shows care and concern, is friendly and approachable, and values students as individual people.[8]

Churches can help young people (and other school personnel who are part of the church) see how they contribute to a caring climate in their school. In addition, churches can broaden the focus of the asset beyond formal schooling to the climate of each classroom and program that the church sponsors. Are these places warm and inviting? Do children and youth feel cared for? How enthusiastic are young people about coming each time? These are only a few of the key questions that can help you evaluate the climate.

Overall, 25 percent of young people say they have asset #5: caring school climate. Twenty-seven percent of all girls report having this asset compared to 22 percent of guys.

ASSET #6:

Parent Involvement in Schooling

A critical key for a young person's academic success is parental involvement. This includes parents who actively participate in the life of the school and those who work to create a positive learning environment at home, ensuring that children and teenagers complete and do their homework well.

Unfortunately, Search Institute researchers discovered that parental involvement drops as a young person gets older. The percentage of young people who say their parents are involved in their education by grade:

Sixth grade	45%
Seventh grade	40%
Eighth grade	32%
Ninth grade	28%
Tenth grade	23%
Eleventh grade	20%
Twelfth grade	17%

Congregations can encourage parents to become more involved in

AN ASSET-BUILDING CHURCH

Creating Intergenerational Relationships

Bethel Lutheran Church in Northfield, Minnesota, created an intergenerational Bible summer school so that adults can learn side by side with children and youth. The asset-building program emphasized forming relationships between children, youth, and adults.

AN ASSET-BUILDING CHURCH

Creating a Caring Neighborhood

North Shore Baptist Church in the Uptown community of North Chicago opens its doors to young men from three neighboring HUD buildings. With the help of staff from After School Action Programs and local residents, the church provides sports activities and educational programming. Youth minister Ezelle Sherrod says one of the most important things about this program is altering the perception young people have of the church. "We wanted the local young people to know we are not just here on Sundays. They don't think churches have a function other than saving souls, but we wanted to make it clear we're there for them in all aspects of life."

their children's schooling by educating the importance of this asset. Researchers have found that parental involvement promotes student success at all grade levels, not just the younger grades.[9]

Some key ways that parents can build this asset are by expressing interest in what their children are doing at school, making sure there is a place to study at home, monitoring the completion of homework, talking about school activities and homework, making sure children attend school, and encouraging children to read.[10]

Ideas for All Ministries to Show Support

● Learn young people's names.

● Get to know one or two young people at a deeper level.

● Go out of your way to greet and talk to young people.

● Smile at young people when you see them.

● Develop programs and activities that support children and young people.

Ideas for Church Nurseries to Show Support

● Hang up photographs of the children in your care along with their names outside the door to your nursery. Update these photos often as children grow.

● Foster consistency by having the same person be present each week. If you struggle with turnover, invest in your church nursery and pay someone well in order to ensure consistent care. This consistent care often is a key reason why families with

young children either stay or leave a church.

● Be sensitive to parents, especially parents of newborns. Many are sleep deprived and are still adjusting to family life with a new child. Find ways to support parents in these situations.

● Make eye contact with the people you work with: the children, the other nursery volunteers, and the parents. Be intentional about smiling and creating a warm, inviting atmosphere.

● Decorate the nursery with areas that are stimulating and soothing to young children. Children need places for exploration and places for winding down.

Ideas for Children's Ministry to Show Support

● Keep track of children's birthdays and other significant dates (such as an adoption arrival date). Send a card on these days.

● Create programming for children that occurs at the same time as other church programming so that parents aren't having to make an extra trip.

● Touch children in supportive ways. Younger children enjoy hugs and snuggling when you read a book, but older children like physical affection too.

● Answer children's questions and take each question seriously, even if a child asks it over and over again.

● Give children time to choose what they want to play. Join in on the play.

Ideas for Youth Ministry to Show Support

- Create mentoring relationships between youth and adults.

- Ask young people for ideas on how they would like to be supported. Implement one or two of those ideas.

- Create a climate in your youth programming that is warm, friendly, welcoming, and accepting of all youth.

- In planning social or fellowship activities, select those that provide youth with lots of opportunities for building relationships with each other and with the adults involved.

- Have interested teenagers of the congregation form a baby-sitting service so parents of young children can have a list of teenagers who would be interested in providing child care.

- Meet during times that best fit teenagers' schedules. For example, some youth groups meet for breakfast once a week at a local restaurant due to the heavy schedules of those involved.

- Have young people design and decorate their own youth room that has a caring, inviting climate. Raise funds if you have to.

For more information on an asset-building perspective on involving parents of youth, see: *Overlooked Allies: How to Involve Parents of Youth* (Nashville: Abingdon, 1997).

AN ASSET-BUILDING CHURCH

Supporting Young People in Many Ways

St. Luke Presbyterian Church in Minnetonka, Minnesota, created a number of activities and programs with the intention of supporting young people through building assets. The congregation

- launched a faith partners program that matched interested adults with interested children. The goal of the program was to form informal relationships.

- created name tags for all the children in the congregation.

- had weekly "stars of the week" that recognized two children in the congregation. Short biographical sketches appeared in the worship bulletin, and the children were introduced to the congregation during the children's service.

- began a monthly common meeting night, providing a catered dinner. Committees met and free child care was offered to parents.

- offered an annual gift-making workshop the first Saturday in December so that first- to sixth-graders could make Christmas presents and wrap them with the help of adults. Children made gifts such as bird feeders, doorstops, tree ornaments, and stationery.

Family Communication
ABOUT FAITH

Search Institute surveys of more than three thousand young people in 561 Christian churches found that one area of positive family communication that's lacking is communication about faith or God. Here are the percentages of sixteen- to eighteen-year-old youth who report each of the following:

38%
Rarely or never talking to mother about faith or God between ages five and twelve

35%
Rarely or never talking to mother about faith or God between ages thirteen and fifteen

56%
Rarely or never talking to father about faith or God between ages five and twelve

63%
Rarely or never talking to father about faith or God between ages thirteen and fifteen

54%
Rarely or never having family devotions between ages five and twelve

64%
Rarely or never having family devotions between ages thirteen and fifteen

Nurturing an Asset-Building Climate

Offering quality programs or activities is not enough to create an asset-building program. Just as important is the climate or atmosphere. Just as comfortable weather adds energy and enthusiasm, a comfortable and safe "climate" in activities for children and youth enhances the asset-building potential of your congregation. If, for example, young people are ignored or teased during activities, they will remember little of the programming content because it is overshadowed by the way they were treated.

Thus, while it's important to plan quality programs, it's just as important to focus on creating a climate in which asset building can flourish. Characteristics of an asset-building climate in a congregation include:

- [ ] **Warmth**—The congregation is friendly and welcoming.

- [ ] **Caring**—Young people feel that people (children, youth, and adults) care about them.

- [ ] **Thinking**—Young people are challenged to think and grow; it's stimulating and interesting to be there.

- [ ] **Valuing**—Young people are valued and respected.

- [ ] **Dealing constructively with conflict**—While some conflict is inevitable in a program, it's important that it be dealt with constructively and not be allowed to fester and infect relationships among the young people and leaders.[11]

Everyone has a role to play in creating a positive climate. The adults who are involved can set a tone of openness and acceptance. Through their attitudes and actions toward each other, young people also contribute to a positive climate. And the whole congregation—in the way members treat children and youth—can also enhance the climate.

One area in which congregations may inadvertently create an unfriendly climate is with newcomers or visitors—particularly if the visitors are not familiar with the congregation's traditions, customs, and norms; or if the visitor is very different from others in the group. These issues are important to address both with leaders and young people, equipping them with the attitudes and skills they need to welcome people who are different from them.

People Bingo

Try to fill up five squares in a row—horizontally, vertically, or diagonally—by finding someone who fits the description in the box. Then write that person's name in the box. If there is a question in parentheses, write the response to that, too. When you fill in five boxes in a row, shout BINGO! (Note: You can't ask the same person to fill in two squares.)

Knows the name of almost everyone in the room.	Likes to fly kites.	Plays an instrument in a band or ochestra.	Has participated in a service project in the past two months.	Takes at least one airplane trip each month.
Is a grandparent. (How many grandchildren?)	Has been on a spiritual retreat in the past two months.	Rides a bus to school or work.	Has had an unusual nickname. (Name it.)	Has been a member of this congregation for at least ten years. (How long?)
Owns a dog. (What's its name?)	Has held an elected office. (What office?)	Has lived in this state all her/his life.	Has become part of this congregation this year.	Usually stays up until midnight or later.
Likes to play table games such as bridge. (Which games?)	Usually gets up before 6 a.m.	Can speak more than two languages. (Which ones?)	Has at least three grandparents still living.	Enjoys listening to rock music. (Favorite artist?)
Has met a president or governor. (Which one?)	Volunteers in a program for children or youth. (Where?)	Likes to babysit or do projects for neighbors.	Is home during the day most of the time.	Likes to play basketball.

Ideas for Family Ministry to Show Support

- Create ways for families to get together to talk about support. Have each family member name the specific ways each family member supports her or him.

- Research how your church currently supports families. Do families feel supportive? Is their enthusiasm high? Which families aren't involved? Why not?

- Invite a parent educator to offer workshops for parents on how to build the support assets, such as communicating positively and effectively with children (asset #2), tips for finding quality child care (asset #5), and fun ways to build family support (asset #1).

- Visit the home of each family in your church to show your support.

- Write about a different family each week in your congregation's newsletter.

- Hold intergenerational family events that bring together members of all ages to socialize and get to know each other as families.

- Give families opportunities to have fun together. Family sports teams, game nights, camping or canoe trips, and dozens of other activities can be great, nonthreatening ways for parents and teenagers to spend time together—particularly if they are noncompetitive.

Ideas for Christian Education to Show Support

- Promote family love and support through the curriculum. Do crafts, games, and other activities to emphasize support.

- Encourage parents to be involved not only in their children's Christian education but also in their children's child care, school, activities, and overall development. Ask parents questions about other aspects of their children's lives, showing interest and encouraging development.

- Find out which young people live in your church neighborhood. Build neighborhood connections, such as taking young people for a walk through the neighborhood in the fall in search of leaves or to do a neighborhood cleanup, picking up litter and trash.

- Create ways for young people to get to know adults in your congregation. For example, find out some of the unique interests and talents of individual adults in your congregation. A carpenter could teach a class on how to build a simple birdhouse and in the process get to know a few names. A gardener could plant seeds with a class and share enthusiasm for growing flowers and vegetables.

- Periodically (perhaps once a year or once a semester) create a family class where you invite the entire family to come. Some classes have separated the time into two blocks: (1) a time for the adults to get to know each other while the children are busy elsewhere, and (2) a time when families do activities together.

Ideas for Intergenerational Ministry to Show Support

- Highlight the schedule of games, concerts, plays, or events that children and teenagers are involved in.

- Form partnerships between congregational adults and children. Encourage them to sit together at worship services and get to know each other's family.

- At all-church functions, plan some easy intergenerational activities that encourage children to get to know other adults in the church. For example, to discourage age-segregation and encourage people to mix more, group participants according to where they live, their favorite colors, or their birth months.

- Match families who have children with those who don't have children to develop mutual support and build asset #3: other caring adults.

- Be sure that people of all ages have opportunities to know each other. Some congregations help people remember each other by providing name tags for everyone.

- Plan games at picnics and other events that are appropriate for all ages, not just for children or those who are physically fit.

- Identify ways to build relationships between people. For example, recruit adults to be classroom readers to read books to children during the Christian education hour. Find teenagers who would be interested in playing guitar or piano for a short musical time with preschoolers.

Ideas for Community Outreach to Show Support

● Link up with the neighborhood in which your congregation is located. Attend neighborhood block parties, and get to know the adults and young people who live near your congregation.

● Bring different sectors of the community together to discuss ways to support families. For example, some communities consider Wednesday night as a time when congregations provide programs for children and youth; schools do not schedule activities on these nights. In other communities, Sunday evenings are set aside as family time, and sports organizations do not schedule games.

● Join with other congregations or community groups to sponsor a survey of developmental assets among young people in your community.[12]

● Get congregational members involved in (or cosponsor) a community mentoring program.

NOTES

1. Eugene C. Roehlkepartain, *The Teaching Church: Moving Christian Education to Center Stage* (Nashville, Abingdon, 1993).

2. Peter L. Benson, Eugene C. Roehlkepartain, and I. Shelby Andress, *Congregations at Crossroads: A National Study of Adults and Youth in The Lutheran Church-Missouri Synod* (Minneapolis: Search Institute, 1995), 16.

3. Silvia M. Bell and Mary D. S. Ainsworth, "Infant Crying and Maternal Responsiveness," in *Child Development and Behavior*, 2d ed., Freda Rebelsky and Lynn Dormon, eds. (New York: Knopf, 1973). Also "Infant Crying and Maternal Responsiveness," Child Development 43, no. 4 (1972): 1171-1190.

4. N. Eisenberg and S. McNally, "Socialization and Mothers' and Adolescents' Empathy-Related Characteristics," Journal of Research on Adolescence 3 (1993): 171-191.

5. Eugene C. Roehlkepartain and Peter L. Benson, *Youth in Protestant Churches: A Special Search Institute Report* (Minneapolis: Search Institute, 1993), 113.

6. A. Talmi, and S. Harter, "Pathways to Better Outcomes: Special Adults as Sources of Support for Young Adolescents" (presented at the biennial meeting of the Society for Research on Adolescence, San Diego, 1998).

7. G.M.H. Pretty, L. Andrewes, and C Collett, "Exploring Adolescents' Sense of Community and Its Relationship to Loneliness," Journal of Community Psychology 22 (1994): 346-358.

8. C. Goodenow, "Classroom Belonging Among Early Adolescent Students: Relationships to Motivation and Achievement," Journal of Early Adolescence 13 (1993): 21-43. Also, C. Goodenow, "The Psychological Sense of School Membership Among Adolescents: Scale Development and Educational Correlates," Psychology in the Schools 30 (1993): 79-90.

9. R.B. Palmer, G.A Dakof, and H.A. Liddle, "Family Processes, Family Interventions, and Adolescent School Problems: A Critical Review and Analysis" in K.L. Alves-Zervos and J.R. Shafer, eds., *Synthesis of Research and Practice: Implications for Achieving School Success for Children at Risk* (Philadelphia: Temple University, National Center on Education in the Inner Cities, 1993), 101-136.

10. Peter C. Scales and Nancy Leffert, *Developmental Assets: A Synthesis of the Scientific Research on Adolescent Development* (Minneapolis: Search Institute, 1999), 36.

11. These same characteristics that contribute to an asset-building climate are also important for nurturing faith in youth. See Eugene C. Roehlkepartain, *The Teaching Church: Moving Christian Education to Center Stage* (Nashville: Abingdon, 1993).

12. Search Institute's survey Profiles of Student Life: Attitudes and Behaviors was designed for this purpose. For information, call 1-800-888-7828.

Empowering Children & Youth

Young people need to feel valued—to know that they are important. They need opportunities to contribute through leadership and service. The empowerment assets highlight this need, focusing on community perceptions of children and youth and opportunities for young people to contribute meaningfully to society. In addition, a sense of empowerment is only possible in an environment where children and youth feel safe.

Empowerment can occur in many ways. Part of it grows out of supportive relationships; when children are noticed and paid attention to, they are more likely to feel valued. In addition, they need opportunities to contribute in acts of service and leadership. Service and leadership are two important themes in asset building, not only because they are assets in and of themselves, but also because they provide important opportunities to nurture many other assets, from building supportive relationships to teaching important social competencies.

Through a wide range of service and social action projects and leadership opportunities, many congregations actively give children and youth these kinds of empowering experiences. Efforts begin by providing a climate that is both physically and emotionally safe—where they feel comfortable risking and possibly failing. In addition, there are dozens of ways to involve children and youth in service and leadership, both inside the congregation as well as in the community.

ASSET #7:

Community Values Children & Youth

A key developmental need for children and youth is to be valued by others and to feel valuable. They grow up knowing their strengths, feeling treated with respect, and sensing they can make a difference in the world. When a community values children and youth, young people feel good about themselves and their skills.

A congregation is an ideal community to value and celebrate children. Some congregations integrate children and youth into worship services on a regular basis to show the importance of people of all ages—including its youngest attendees. Others celebrate an annual children's Sabbath and a youth Sunday in which young people are given valuable, meaningful ways to participate.

Yet another key factor in the way a congregation values young people is the way adults view children and youth. A national study by Public Agenda found that adults have negative views of young people, particularly teenagers. The researchers write: "When asked what first comes to their minds when they think about today's teenagers, two-thirds of Americans (67 percent) immediately reach for negative adjectives such as 'rude,' 'irresponsible,' and 'wild.' Only a handful (12 percent) describe teenagers positively, using terms such as 'smart' or 'helpful.' "[1]

So it shouldn't be surprising that only 20 percent of all young people report having asset #7: community values children and youth. Girls more likely than guys report having this asset—a critical year seems to be the eighth grade. While 22 percent of eighth-grade girls report having this asset, only 10 percent of eighth-grade boys do.

ASSET #8:

Children & Youth as Resources

Children and youth who are given useful roles feel they have some control over their environment and that they have something worth contributing. Adults and teachers can encourage learning and development through involving children and youth in age-appropriate tasks. Even with children as young as eighteen months, adults can select a task for a child to do in which success is likely. The adult can include the child in the planning of the task, make sure the child can complete the task easily, divide the task into child-sized portions, and encourage and reinforce the child's efforts. Through this process, a child can feel valued and empowered.

Giving young people meaningful roles also impacts the choices they make in other areas of their lives. Seventh-graders who helped plan alcohol-free activities such as roller-skating outings or open gyms—compared with youth who either simply attended those events or did not participate at all—were significantly less likely to report using alcohol during the previous year. The effects were stronger for young people who already had used alcohol during the sixth grade, suggesting that youth who are at risk may especially benefit from empowerment.[2]

Overall, only 25 percent of all young people surveyed by Search Institute report being seen as a resource. While 37 percent of sixth-grade girls say they have this asset, only 20 percent of twelfth-grade girls report having this asset. This same decline occurs with boys—34 percent of sixth-graders saying they have this asset compared with 19 percent of twelfth-graders.

Churches are a natural place for young people to develop leadership skills. In fact, many adult leaders report that their early leadership experiences were in the church. Yet many young people don't see their churches doing well at involving them as leaders. One Search Institute study found that only 43 percent of youth in Protestant churches said their church did a good or excellent job of developing their leadership skills.[3] Another study found that 19 percent of youth in one denomination said their church involved youth in decision making.[4]

ASSET #9:

Service to Others

Service to others is an empowerment asset because children and youth (like adults) find that giving to other people carries rewards. "The benefits of including children as providers of service extend beyond today," write the authors of *Children as Volunteers.* "In a very real sense, when we involve them as volunteers, we are preparing our youth to become active, responsible, caring citizens."[5]

Parents begin instilling in their infants the asset of service by focusing on the baby and meeting her or his needs. Children rarely develop the asset of service unless they have experienced the care, love, and support of others and have been taught that the world revolves around all people, not just them. As children become toddlers, parents and adults can model this asset by serving and helping others outside of the family. Gradually the family can include the child in service.

Finding volunteer opportunities that are meaningful for both adults

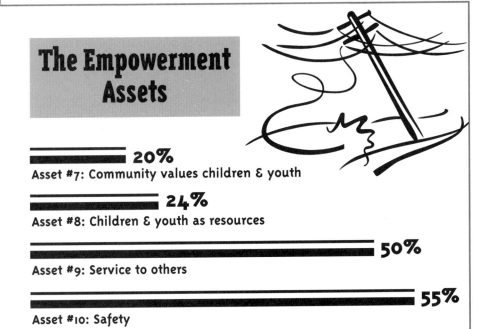

The Empowerment Assets

20%
Asset #7: Community values children & youth

24%
Asset #8: Children & youth as resources

50%
Asset #9: Service to others

55%
Asset #10: Safety

and children can be difficult, however. Activities such as re-roofing the house may empower an adult but will overwhelm a four-year-old. Congregations that create service projects that are geared to the developmental readiness of children are offering a great opportunity for children and their families.

What makes service projects empowering for children and youth? Researchers have found six essential components. Young people need to

- have opportunities to reflect about the meaning of the activity.
- do the actual work and not just observe.
- work with accepting adults who don't criticize their efforts.
- have important responsibilities.
- sense that they can make a contribution.
- have the freedom to explore their own interests and develop their own ideas.[6]

Not only is engaging young people in service to others an asset, it also builds many of the other assets as well. Researchers have found that engaging in effective service activities can build positive values, strengthen positive identity, and enhance a commitment to learning.[7]

Search Institute research finds that 50 percent of all young people report having this asset. However, there are some important differences. First, there is a wide gap between girls and boys. While 55 percent of all girls say they have asset #9: service to others, only 45

percent of all guys do.

In addition, young people who are involved in a faith community are much more likely than other youth to report having this asset (58 percent versus 34 percent). This difference likely reflects the emphasis that many churches place on serving others—and the fact that other researchers consistently find that one of the most common places for young people to serve others is through a religious institution.

Many organizations offer service projects including Group Workcamps (1-800-774-3838) and Habitat for Humanity (1-800-422-4828).

ASSET #10:

Safety

Children and youth who feel safe are more likely to feel valued and able to make a difference than those whose safety is threatened. Growing up in an unsafe or violent environment also shapes the choices children and youth make. For example, research shows that young people who grow up in violent families or violent communities are more likely to abuse alcohol or drugs.[8] That's why creating environments where children and youth are physically and emotionally safe is an important asset-building task.

Children and youth grow up feeling safe and secure if they feel able to learn more about themselves, other people, and the world. Young children who are allowed to slowly process the ordinary fears that occur while growing up are more apt to feel good about themselves. Those who are pushed and whose fears are

dismissed often feel ashamed and begin to think the world is a scary place.

As elementary-age children and high school youth spend less time with their parents and more time with friends, they can often feel overwhelmed with the complex life experiences they may face. Although young people need close friendships, they also need close relationships with their parents who can guide them with the feelings that arise from new experiences. Almost one in five middle school youth and one in ten high school youth say they have been personally victimized. As many as 33 percent of middle school youth say they worry about becoming victims.[9]

Even young children may experience unsafe conditions, which greatly affects their school attendance and performance. Researchers who studied two hundred five- and six-year-olds found that children who were hit, kicked, picked on, or talked to unkindly were more likely to dislike school and more likely to stay home from school.[10]

Although Search Institute research reveals that 55 percent of all young people say they feel safe, a wide discrepancy exists between guys and girls. Guys are much more likely to feel safe than girls. Overall, 63 percent of guys compared to 47 percent of girls report having this asset. The widest gap occurs in twelfth grade when 80 percent of guys and only 57 percent of girls say they feel safe.

It is important to note that safety is the only asset that religiously active youth report slightly *less* than

Providing Safety in Relationships

Marilyn Sharpe, former confirmation director at Mount Olivet Lutheran Church in Minneapolis, went through an extensive process for establishing her congregation's policies and procedures for "the care of children and vulnerable adults" that seek to place safeguards against physical, sexual, and emotional abuse. Some of her suggestions include:

● **Minimize or eliminate time alone.** The greatest danger lies in relationships where one adult spends time alone with one child. As wonderful as these times can be for forming relationships, they can also be the most damaging. Sharpe recommends never having one child and one adult together. Furthermore, it's best to always have more than one adult.

An additional precaution is to have people meet in public places, such as the congregational facilities. Encourage one-to-one interaction during congregational activities, such as eating together at picnics or congregational meals and sitting together during worship. If people want to do activities together away from the congregational site, such as go out to eat or to a ballgame, encourage them to pair up with others. Following the activity, have the kids taken home first so that one adult is never alone in a car with a young person.

● **Be sure you know participating adults.** Sharpe says sexual predators may come to a congregation if they hear it is focusing on intergenerational relationships. For this reason she encourages the policy that someone needs to be active in the congregation at least six months before participating in a planned adult-youth relationship.

● **Set clear ground rules and expectations.** Youth, parents, and others in the congregation (whether or not they are in an intentional mentoring relationship) need to have a shared understanding of what is acceptable and what is not acceptable in adult-youth relationships. Some appropriate ground rules include:

• Have clear guidelines for appropriate and inappropriate touching.

• No secrets are acceptable between a young person and the adult (such as an adult saying, "Let's just have this be our little secret"). If, however, a young person reveals abuse or neglect at home, that issue should be reported to appropriate authorities (the police) and/or to the congregation's senior clergy.

• If an adult-youth pair wants to do something together away from the congregation, they should team up with others for the activity.

● **Connect families with the adults.** It's important for parents to know and communicate with the adults who are spending time with their children. Provide opportunities for them to get together and build relationships.

● **Screen adults, particularly for individual relationships.** If there is little chance that an adult will spend time alone with one youth, screening may not be needed. But as the opportunities for one-to-one time alone increase, the level of screening also needs to increase. Thorough background checks are appropriate if you expect an adult to spend time alone with individual young people.

One of the problems, Sharpe says, is that sexual predators appear, on the surface, to have many of the qualities of a great asset builder. They tend to be great listeners. They know what's important to kids. And they meet kids on their own terms. But then they cross the line and violate the young person's trust, innocence, and body.

Once adult-youth relationships have begun forming, don't ignore them. Periodically check to see how each relationship is going, and watch for warning signs.

● **Have a clear procedure for dealing with problems.** Make it clear that anyone who believes one of the ground rules has been broken must report the violation. Intervene quickly if you see or hear about any warning signs that a relationship may not be healthy.

● **Get more information.** For additional information on creating a safe youth program, see Jack Crabtree, *Better Safe Than Sued: Keeping Out of Trouble in Youth Ministry* (Loveland, CO: Group, 1998).

Note: These suggestions do not represent legal advice. In developing a congregational policy, it is important to seek the services of knowledgeable legal counsel.

AN ASSET-BUILDING CONGREGATION

Empowering Youth for Leadership

Each summer the First Chinese Baptist Church in San Francisco sponsors a day camp for children in the Chinatown community. About one hundred children attend; most of the leadership is provided by youth group members. Youth leader Jerald Choy says the day camp is where the youth "first learn to be more responsible as part of the church."

The program's success is partly due to its progressive training structure, which is based on experience. The first year, kids are counselors in training. The next year, they become junior counselors. "By the time they've been in the program three years, they're ready to be senior counselors," Choy says. "They can take a whole group of kids and plan the program with the junior counselors and counselors in training."[11]

nonreligious or inactive youth. The reason for this finding is unclear and would require greater research to uncover. However, it may relate to the gender difference: girls (who feel less safe in general) are more likely than boys to participate in religious programs and activities.

Ideas for All Ministries to Empower Young People

- Ask for young people's ideas on making your congregation a better place—and act on their ideas.

- Childproof *all* rooms of your church to make them safe, inviting places for young children.

- Create service projects that empower children and youth in addition to adults.

- Create at least two youth positions on each congregational committee.

- Include young people in the planning and implementation of congregation-wide functions, such as church picnics and fall kickoff Sunday.

Ideas for Church Nurseries to Empower Children

- Empower children by making activities accessible to children. Have coat pegs hung at a level where toddlers can reach their own coats. Place age-appropriate toys close to infants and toddlers where they can reach them.

- Create keepsakes that have either children's handprints or footprints on them.

- Give parents extra strokes from time to time. Show parents how much you value their roles.

- Make photo displays of children who attend your nursery. Make one photo display at adult eye level and one at infant eye level.

- Create simple service projects for older infants and toddlers. For example, young children can pick up toys and place them in a large bucket at the end of your nursery time. Emphasize how they are helping and serving. Toddlers also can show picture books to an infant who is being held by an adult.

Ideas for Children's Ministry to Empower Children

- Value each child's opinions and suggestions when asking questions.

- Explain to children how they can be "cheerful givers" on a regular basis by designating a portion of their allowances for church and charities. Distribute specially designed envelopes to encourage them in this ministry.

- Give children useful, meaningful roles. For example, children can choose the music and the games for a children's ministry event.

- Find service projects that challenge and empower children. For example, fourth- to sixth-graders can decorate buckets or containers for medicine kits and write a card or letter to be delivered with each kit. Kindergartners to third-graders can inventory items for medicine kits and assemble them.

Meaningful Service Projects

FOR CHILDREN AND YOUTH

H ere are some ideas for developing age-appropriate, worthwhile activities that children and youth can do to serve others.

Ideas for Three- to Five-Year-Olds

☐ Take preschoolers shopping for light items they can carry and then distribute. A senior residential home may enjoy receiving boxes of tissues, stamps, envelopes, and toilet paper.

☐ Have preschoolers make a scheduled visit to your pastor. They can bring personalized gifts, such as pictures they've drawn or a plant they have put into a pot they've decorated. Talk about how pastors need visitors, too, and shouldn't have to do all the visiting themselves.

☐ Contact parents who have recently sent a freshman off to college or moved a child into an apartment. Set a date when kids can visit, and provide a small gift that children can present, such as freshly cut flowers or homemade chocolate chip cookies. Preschoolers can be welcome guests to a new empty nest.

Ideas for Six- to Nine-Year-Olds

☐ Plan a sock-it-away fund-raiser. First, ask kids as a group to choose between two or three charities they would like to give money to. Then have each child bring in one sock (that will be returned) with loose change that they've saved over a period of time.

☐ Provide the opportunity for a toy swap. First, alert parents and ask for their permission before you do this. Then encourage children each to bring in four or five toys they no longer use and would be willing to trade. Talk about how they can help recycle toys and find new treasures for themselves as well.

☐ In the fall, have children help adult volunteers plant bulbs in the yards of homebound or bedridden church members. Likewise, in the spring children can help plant seeds and start gardens for people.

Ideas for Ten- to Twelve-Year-Olds

☐ Have children participate in a "read-a-thon" by getting sponsors and setting individual goals to raise money for an important cause for literacy and reading. Children can sign up to read books from the library or books of the Bible.

☐ Contact a local service agency to offer children's help to wrap items that have been purchased for families with low incomes. Service agencies often wrap items once they have been collected. With supervision, children in your congregation can help with the wrapping.

☐ Visit your church nursery or toddler room to have children hunt for puzzle pieces, game pieces, and other missing items. Children can also tidy the area by grouping similar toys together and putting clothes back on dolls.

Ideas for Thirteen- to Fifteen-Year-Olds

☐ Encourage youth to rehearse and present a traveling puppet show to the children of your church. One presentation could be in the nursery, one during a recreation program, and one in Christian education classes.

☐ With youth, plan a Christmas tree collection after the Christmas season. With adult supervision, have kids trim off branches to create bush and shrub mulch for the spring. The tree trunk can be chopped into firewood to give away for free.

☐ Set aside some time for youth to create homemade birthday cards to send to church members on their birthdays.

Ideas for Sixteen- to Eighteen-Year-Olds

☐ Ask teenagers to host a "senior prom" at your church. Young people can organize and publicize the dress-up dance for people over the age of sixty. Encourage the generations to work together, deciding on what music to play and what refreshments to serve. During the dance, encourage teenagers and seniors to dance together.

☐ Offer your young people's budding talent to paint murals over graffiti-covered walls in your city. With permission from the landowners or city administrators, have youth plan the murals and paint their designs.

☐ Offer a shuttle service so that all people in this age group with disabilities or illness attend church events.

Increasing the Visibility

OF CHILDREN AND YOUTH

One of the reasons children and youth sometimes don't feel empowered is that they are invisible to many adults in the congregation. Plans are made and activities are led with little or no recognition that young people will—or could—be participating. Adults greet other adults without saying a word to the child or teenager who is accompanying her or his parent. Many of the strategies for developing an asset framework will increase child and youth visibility. Some specific ideas to try:

☐ If the congregation prepares name tags for adults to wear during congregational activities, prepare similar ones for children and youth.

☐ Highlight the activities and accomplishments of children and youth to the whole congregation.

☐ If the congregation has a newsletter, include children's ministry, nursery, and youth news and activities (even if you have a separate newsletter for young people).

☐ Give children and youth opportunities to make announcements, serve as ushers, and perform other tasks that make them visible in the larger community of faith.

☐ Highlight activities and programs for children and youth as congregational activities. For example, when youth go on a workcamp or other service trip, recognize them as representatives of the whole congregation, not just the youth program.

☐ Whenever you ask children and youth to lead, train them in what they can expect and how they can be effective in their role. Provide ongoing support and guidance.

☐ Include young people in your youth programming leadership team. This gives youth a sense of ownership. They begin to see programs as something that they do with adults, not something adults do for them.

☐ Provide opportunities for children and youth to serve in leadership roles in the larger congregation. This could include serving on committees, providing leadership in worship and other activities, organizing special events for the congregation, and leading programs and activities for younger children.

☐ Offer regular service opportunities that older children and youth can plan and lead. For younger children, offer service opportunities that give them a voice in planning and implementation.

- Periodically ask children about their fears and what would help them feel more safe. Implement their suggestions.

- Train adults who work with children to view children in positive ways and interact with them in ways that are empowering to both adults and children.

Ideas for Youth Ministry to Empower Youth

- Provide frequent, ongoing opportunities for young people to engage in service to others and to reflect on their experiences.

- Ask youth to be leaders at worship services. They can do readings or serve as ushers.

- Provide young people with leadership roles in the youth ministry and the church. Build their leadership skills, and support and encourage them to develop as strong leaders.[12]

- Ensure that young people are always safe in your programming by selecting responsible drivers.

- Have young people plan and participate in youth events. Allow them to do their part with the assistance of adults.

- Carefully screen people who have lots of contact with individual youth to ensure that young people are safe.

- Create activities that encourage young people to empower each other. For example, cut out a construction paper star for each young person, and pin one to each back. Have young people take turns writing one thing on each star they admire about each person.

Ideas for Family Ministry to Empower Young People

- Ask families to be involved in leadership together. For example, families can read Scripture in dialogue, light candles together, or provide special music.

- Design service opportunities that allow parents and children to spend time together rather than apart.

- Hold a celebration each year to honor the families and children in your congregation. For example, have an ice-cream social.

- Ask families for their input about your family ministry events. Most families are busy, so create events that fit their needs and schedules.

- Create family service pairs. Once a month have one family pair go to the other family's home to do needed fix-up projects around the apartment or house. The next month switch—have the family who received help go to the other family's home. In this way families benefit from the help and also give help.

AN ASSET-BUILDING CONGREGATION

Empowering Children

Bethlehem Lutheran Church in Minneapolis offers a Parents Day Out every December. Junior and senior high students in the youth group provide child care and activities for children ages six months to sixth grade. The teenagers help the kids bake cookies and make cards for homebound congregational members. Then preschoolers to third-graders deliver the cookies and cards while singing carols. Adults and older teenagers take the fourth- to sixth-graders shopping to buy toys for children in low-income families. The money for the toys is provided by fund-raisers sponsored by the fourth-graders in the congregation.

A few years ago one member of the congregation vowed to match whatever the class raised. When the class raised four hundred dollars, the congregation found a corporate sponsor to match gifts. American Express Financial Services now matches the three thousand dollars the fourth-grade class raises annually to buy these toys.

Ideas for Christian Education to Empower Young People

● Give children and youth each a turn to plan and decorate a classroom bulletin board. Challenge young people to be creative.

● Invite children and youth to draw designs for a congregational T-shirt or sweatshirt or to draw designs for calendars, stationery, or notepads. Sell these items as fund-raisers.

● Provide extender wands and step stools so young children can reach light switches and have more accessibility to things they need. Create classrooms that are inviting and young people friendly. Middle and high school young people often like beanbag chairs and similar comfortable places to sit.

● Have classrooms take turns serving each other. For example, high school youth can play games with children. Fifth-graders can read stories to kindergartners. Preschoolers can sing lullabies to babies.

Ideas for Intergenerational Ministry to Empower Young People

● Include children and youth in congregation-wide service projects and work trips.

● Provide opportunities for children and youth to serve in leadership roles in the larger congregation. This could include serving on committees, providing leadership in worship, organizing a special event for the congregation, and leading an activity during a program for younger children.

● When providing refreshments at congregation-wide events, be sure they are appropriate for both children and adults. For example, serve juice as well as coffee. Have fruit and cookies.

● Create an intergenerational choir that sings periodically in worship (perhaps once a month or four times a year). Encourage people of all ages to sing in this choir, and extend a special invitation to families to sing together in this choir.

● When you have intergenerational discussion groups, first talk about language issues. Will everyone go by first names? Is the term "kids" offensive to some participants?

Ideas for Community Outreach to Empower Young People

● Offer leadership development opportunities to children and young people in the community.

● Invite young people from the community to participate in congregation-sponsored service projects.

● Challenge messages in the media that stereotype children and youth or portray them as problems. Affirm stories that reflect an asset-building perspective on children and youth. Send letters to the editor, meet with editorial boards, and take other appropriate action.

● Become an advocate and partner in community efforts to improve safety for children and youth.

● Involve community youth in planning all activities and programs designed for them. Involve parents and children in planning family activities and programs.

NOTES

1. Steve Farkas and Jean Johnson, *Kids These Days: What Americans Really Think About the Next Generation* (New York: Public Agenda, 1997), 8.

2. K.A. Komro et al., "Peer-Planned Social Activities for Preventing Alcohol Use Among Young Adolescents," Journal of School Health 66 (1996): 328-334.

3. Eugene C. Roehlkepartain and Peter L. Benson, *Youth in Protestant Churches: A Special Search Institute Report* (Minneapolis: Search Institute, 1993), 113.

4. Peter L. Benson, Eugene C. Roehlkepartain, and I. Shelby Andress, *Congregations at Crossroads: A National Study of Adults and Youth in The Lutheran Church-Missouri Synod* (Minneapolis: Search Institute, 1995), 23.

5. Susan J. Ellis, Anne Weisbord, and Katherine H. Noyes, *Children as Volunteers: Preparing for Community Service* (Philadelphia: Energize, 1991), 1.

6. J.P. Hill, *Participatory Education and Youth Development in Secondary Schools* (Philadelphia: Research for Better Schools, ERIC Document Reproduction Service No. ED 242 701, 1983).

7. Summarized in Eugene C. Roehlkepartain, Thomas Bright, and Beth Margolis-Rupp, *An Asset Builder's Guide to Service-Learning* (Minneapolis: Search Institute, 2000).

8. A.C. Fick and S.M. Thomas, "Growing Up in a Violent Environment: Relationship to Health-Related Beliefs and Behaviors," Youth & Society 27, no. 2 (1995): 136-147.

9. M.J. Nolin, E. Davies, and K. Chandler, *Student Victimization at School: Statistics in Brief* (Rockville, MD: Westat, 1995).

10. G.W. Ladd, B.J. Kochenderfer, and C.C. Coleman, "Classroom Peer Acceptance, Friendship, and Victimization: Distinct Relational Systems that Contribute Uniquely to Children's School Adjustment," Child Development 68 (1997): 1181-1197.

11. From Eugene C. Roehlkepartain, *Youth Ministry in City Churches* (Loveland, CO: Group, 1989), 223.

12. For suggestions on how to strengthen youth leadership from an asset-building perspective, see David Adams et al., *An Asset Builder's Guide to Youth Leadership* (Minneapolis: Search Institute, 1999).

Setting Boundaries & Expectations

For healthy development, clear and enforced boundaries need to complement support and empowerment. Young people need clear signals about what behavior is expected and what is unacceptable—what is "in bounds" and what is "out of bounds." Once set, boundaries need to be monitored and enforced with appropriate and consistent discipline. These boundaries begin at home and should extend to other settings where young people spend their time, including the congregation, neighborhood, school, jobs, and places of entertainment.

Similar to setting boundaries is the importance of people having high expectations for young people. These high expectations can challenge children and youth to excel and can enhance their sense of being capable. While high expectations are typically associated with education, the same principle applies to expectations in other areas of life: high expectations for how children and youth live out social relationships, how they spend their time, and how they live out their beliefs.

Some churches are reluctant to place boundaries or expectations on children and youth for fear of scaring them away. The framework of assets challenges congregations to begin articulating boundaries and expectations, not in a punitive, condemning way, but as a positive way of passing on wisdom to young people.

The boundaries-and-expectations assets raise provocative questions for those who work with children and youth in congregations. Mark Conway, a youth worker from Annunciation Catholic Church in Minneapolis, described his congregation's policy that any young person who becomes a peer minister must agree to be completely chemically free all year. He believes that these youth are leaders in the youth group and should model responsible behavior

everywhere, not just while in the congregation.

Boundaries and expectations are an essential part of the life, and they are also part of faithful discipleship for Christians. They are a way of offering young people guidance and direction in the choices they make. They also challenge churches to expect the best from children, teenagers, and families.

ASSET #11:

Family Boundaries

Children and teenagers need to know how to act and how not to act. They need clear instructions—not conflicting messages—from parents and other caregivers. In the first half of this century, most American babies were raised on a schedule. They had to wait to be fed until the next scheduled feeding time. Today we know that it is important to respond immediately to infants' cries and to set boundaries and expectations sensitive to children's changing needs. By the time they are three months old, many babies have established a regular daily rhythm. Sleeping through the night often is one of the first boundaries parents and caregivers can set for the child.

Research shows the importance of supervision, monitoring, and boundary setting. In a study of more than eight hundred fifth- to ninth-graders, researchers found that young people who had less adult supervision than other young people were more susceptible to peer pressure and thus more likely to participate in antisocial activity.[1]

Churches can play a pivotal role in educating, training, and supporting families to build this asset. Because so many mixed messages exist in our culture about critical issues, such as alcohol and other drug use, sex, use of money, and other hot topics, many parents are confused about how to set and enforce appropriate boundaries. Many want guid-

ance from the church to see how boundaries and values work hand in hand.

Search Institute researchers found that 43 percent of the sixth- to twelfth-grade youth surveyed report having asset #11: family boundaries. Yet girls are more likely to say they have this asset than boys. While 46 percent of girls report having this asset, only 40 percent of boys do.

ASSET #12:

School Boundaries

Children and teenagers need to know what constitutes acceptable behavior and what to expect when they venture outside the family. When children are in child care, pre-

school, school, or other settings outside the home, they need to know the boundaries and expectations pertinent to each situation. Researchers have found that warm and supportive school environments with consistent boundaries and expectations help young people internalize educational norms and standards. These boundaries may also buffer the effects of negative peer pressure.[2]

While the school-boundaries asset and research focus on boundaries in a school setting, the basic principle is relevant to congregations, too. Christian education classes are more effective when children and youth are given clear rules and consequences. The same is true for church nurseries, children's ministry programs, youth ministry programs, family ministry programs, and any other program of the church.

When asked about boundaries in their schools, 46 percent of young people said they had asset #12. Girls are more likely to have this asset than boys. While 49 percent of girls report having this asset, only 43 percent of boys do.

ASSET #13:

Neighborhood Boundaries

When children and teenagers are playing with others in the neighborhood, they need to know the boundaries and expectations involved in playing with others. They need to understand areas of neighborhood and community that are off limits. They need neighbors who keep an eye out for them and reinforce healthy boundaries.

Neighborhoods with strong social

The Boundaries & Expectations Assets

Asset #11: Family boundaries — 43%

Asset #12: School boundaries — 46%

Asset #13: Neighborhood boundaries — 46%

Asset #14: Adult role models — 27%

Asset #15: Positive peer influence — 60%

Asset #16: High expectations — 41%

AN ASSET-BUILDING CONGREGATION

Setting High Expectations

Congregations can set high expectations for youth. Mount Gideon Missionary Baptist Church in St. Louis, Missouri, sponsors a program to recognize outstanding young people in the community through membership in Youth on a Mission. The program is open to youth who

- maintain a grade-point average of at least 3.25,

- submit a letter of reference from both a teacher and a home church pastor, and

- participate in a monthly community service project.

The rigorous membership requirements are an incentive for local youth to work hard in their school, congregation, and community. One particularly popular aspect of the program is the annual ball, where the youth are honored with a formal introduction to the assembled gathering.

controls provide positive role models and more effective networking between parents, their children's friends, and other parents. When neighbors are willing to get involved in boundary setting for children and youth, parents and adults feel supported in their own disciplinary efforts, which builds asset #11: family boundaries.[3]

The neighborhood-boundaries asset has two major implications for the church. First, it calls congregations to reflect on how everyone in the church (not just the parents, ministry volunteers, and staff, but everyone) has a responsibility to know, monitor, and enforce boundaries in church. These may include respect for each other, respect for property, and appropriate language. This congregational expectation not only creates a healthy sense of "neighborhood" in the church, but it also helps members practice how to appropriately set and enforce healthy boundaries in their own neighborhoods.

Second, churches can become part of setting and enforcing neighborhood boundaries in their geographic neighborhoods by linking with the people who live nearby. Neighborhood boundaries are most effective when a caring sense of community already exists (see asset #4: caring neighborhood). And when trust is built, people are more willing to discuss difficult issues, which some boundaries may raise.

Search Institute researchers have found that 46 percent of all young people say they have asset #13: neighborhood boundaries. However, a wide gap exists between girls and guys. While 56 percent of girls report having this asset, only 45 per-

cent of guys do.

Sometimes we think of declining neighborhood boundaries as an "urban issue." However, Search Institute's surveys find little difference in this asset across different sizes and types of communities. Youth in large cities are almost as likely to report having this asset as young people who live in suburbs, small towns, or on farms.[4]

ASSET #14:

Adult Role Models

An important way children and teenagers learn to act and interact with others is by watching and imitating the adults around them: parents, adults in the congregation, Sunday school teachers, youth workers, and children's workers. That's why it's important for children and youth to have adults who set good examples and model positive, responsible behavior.

Congregations are full of potentially wonderful adult role models. However, many children know only a handful of adults in the church, and some adults may know none of the children. That's why it's important for children and youth to get to know the adults in their church—even the adults with whom they would otherwise have no contact. While it's easy for young people to get to know Sunday school teachers and youth advisors, it's not always easy for them to get to know other adults.

At St. Luke Presbyterian Church in Minnetonka, Minnesota, the congregation created a program called Faith Partners to link young people with an adult in the congregation.

Each fall, interested children, youth, and adults sign up for the program. Then they are randomly matched. During the school year, each pair gets to know each other by sitting together during worship services, going out for an ice-cream cone, checking in with each other, and talking during fellowship times.

Each fall, new pairs are introduced so that children and youth can get to know a large number of adults over the course of a number of years. Some pairs continue doing things together long after each program year ends. In the process, children and youth find adult role models to emulate.

Search Institute research has found that only 27 percent of all young people say they have asset #14: adult role models. Girls are more likely than boys to have this asset. While 31 percent of girls report having adult role models, only 23 percent of guys do.

ASSET #15:

Positive Peer Influence

In the same way that positive adult role models are important for children and youth, so too are relationships with peers who model positive behavior. Although these relationships change over the course of childhood and adolescence, research has shown that close peer relationships are an essential part of social development.[5]

Researchers have found that the biggest influence on the way children play with other children is the relationship children have with their parents.[6] Children and teenagers learn interpersonal skills from their parents, and the quality of the relationship between the child and the parent influences the child's skill in getting along with others.

Once young people become teenagers, their perceptions of what their peers are doing greatly influences their behavior. Researchers have found that these perceptions are often inaccurate. For example, teenagers who begin smoking tend to think that many of their peers smoke, more than the number who actually do.[7]

Many churches emphasize peer pressure, although some overemphasize the effects of negative peer pressure rather than giving young people the skills they need to form relationships with peers who influence them in positive ways. It's true that children and teenagers need to know about negative peer pressure, but they also need the skills to act in caring, positive ways toward their peers. And they need to know how to choose friends who bring out the best in them.

Search Institute researchers have found that 60 percent of all young people say they have asset #15: positive peer influence. In general, young people are twice as likely to say their peers model responsible behavior (60 percent) as they are to say they have positive adult role models (27 percent).

AN ASSET-BUILDING CHURCH

An Eighty-Year-Old Artistic Mentor

When Broadway United Methodist Church in Indianapolis decided to create a music endowment to provide violin lessons to neighborhood young people, a violinist from the congregation offered to teach the youth for free. She is eighty years old.

In addition to being used for violin lessons, the fifty-thousand-dollar endowment goes toward the purchase of violins for the young people. Inspired by the generosity of church members, the church security guard decided to be a mentor in his own way. He chose to donate his modest salary for scholarships that the church awards to neighborhood youth.

ASSET #16:

High Expectations

Children and youth need to grow at their own pace and to develop their unique talents. This requires that adults understand basic information about child and adolescent development, such as the different rates at which young people grow. Adults who are sensitive to child and adolescent development issues are more apt to have realistic expectations and bring out the best in young people.

Having adults who expect young people to do their best is important for children and youth. These adults include parents, teachers, Sunday school teachers, children's ministry volunteers, and youth workers. In fact, high expectations may have a great impact on a young person's achievement.[8]

Congregations should have high expectations of children and youth, too. Christian education, confirmation classes, children's ministry, the church nursery, youth ministry, and other church programs all set standards and have expectations for young people. How high should these expectations be? Expectations can be compared to a helium balloon. When there's too little helium, the balloon falls to the floor. When there's too much, the balloon breaks. With the right amount of helium, the balloon flies high. And a child holding onto the balloon string, stretches upward to keep it taut, while keeping the balloon in sight. Similarly, expectations should make youth stretch upward, all the while being able to keep their goals in sight.

In their attempts to ensure that children and teenagers have fun, make friends, and come back to church, some congregations forget how important it is to challenge young people and have high expectations for them. Several years ago a Search Institute study of more than three thousand young people in six major denominations found that only 42 percent of those surveyed said that their church challenges their thinking. Only 49 percent of the young people said they learned a lot in their church.[9] Furthermore, inactive youth were three times as likely as active youth to say it's boring (24 percent versus 7 percent).[10]

Search Institute researchers have found that 41 percent of all young people say they have asset #16: high expectations, which focuses on expectations that young people will do well in school. How would young people respond if we asked whether they experienced high expectations to learn about and grow in faith?

Ideas for All Ministries to Set Boundaries and Expectations

- Show connections between the boundaries-and-expectations assets and the positive-values assets. Values provide a framework for setting boundaries. For example, valuing honesty (asset #29) means that telling the truth is an important boundary to follow.

- Meet with adults and talk about how to increase comfort levels in upholding boundaries with congregational children who aren't accompanied by their families.

- Use crowd breakers, icebreakers, and community-building games to encourage friendships between children and emphasize the importance of asset #15: positive peer influence.

- Create a code of conduct for worship services. What do you expect of children and teenagers when they attend services? What do you expect of parents who bring infants and toddlers to services?

- Expect children to learn more about your faith tradition and its teachings. Use thought-provoking activities to encourage them to learn more about the Bible and your faith's heritage.

Ideas for Church Nurseries to Set Boundaries and Expectations

- Distract young children from inappropriate behavior. Child development experts say that the time to begin setting limits on children is between seven and one-half and ten months of age. Before that, infants are not capable of breaking rules consciously.

- Make boundaries simple and few. For example, have rules such as these: No biting. Help others. Use your inside voice.

- When identifying boundaries, try to keep an even number of positive and negative rules so that the list of boundaries isn't a long list of noes.

- Create and post a pictorial list of boundaries. Point to the corresponding picture when a boundary has been broken, emphasizing how it's a nursery rule without singling out the individual child.

● Provide training regarding child development issues and techniques for nursery workers so that they can become experts regarding the healthy development of the children in their care.

Ideas for Children's Ministry to Set Boundaries and Expectations

● Post rules and talk about them from day one of your program.

● Educate parents about child development issues. Do this through newsletters, parent training sessions, and meetings. Offer free child care for training sessions and meetings to make it easier for parents to attend.

● Make friendship bracelets with children. School-age children can make friendship bracelets by stringing beads with letters of the alphabet printed on them.

● Tell children how to act when they misbehave. For example, say, "Don't scream when you get mad. With your inside voice say, 'I'm mad.' "

● Monitor how adult volunteers interact with children. Encourage them to interact with children in positive ways, and remind them that they are adult role models.

● Find ways for children of different ages to have fun together. Older children can read stories to younger children, for example.

Ideas for Youth Ministry to Set Boundaries and Expectations

● Establish clear expectations and ground rules for youth who participate in activities, including how they treat each other and how they treat property.

● Include youth in setting clear rules and consequences. Periodically discuss boundaries as a group to see if any need to be updated.

● Insist that all adult volunteers in youth programs and activities be positive role models for youth.

● Introduce young people to many adults in the congregation. Ask the adults to share their faith and life stories with the young people.

● Have meetings and lessons to teach about positive peer influence. Emphasize how young people can be good friends and how they can find friends who influence them in positive ways.

● Set high expectations for how you want young people to act and what you want them to learn.

For more information on an asset-building perspective to help set boundaries in youth ministry, see Kathleen M. Sorensen, *Setting Boundaries With Youth: How to Discipline with Understanding* (Nashville, TN: Abingdon, 1998).

AN ASSET-BUILDING CHURCH

Expecting More From Service

Service projects are the norm at Heritage Baptist Church in Cartersville, Georgia, and so are the high expectations that go along with them. Minister of Christian education Eileen Campbell-Reed works hard to instill in teenagers a real sensitivity toward the needs of the children they work with through a children's shelter. The youth group has an ongoing relationship with Flowering Branch, a shelter for children who have been removed from their homes and are awaiting placement.

The youth group volunteers at the shelter at least six to eight times a year. Campbell-Reed also encourages relationships to deepen by having the youth include the children from the shelter at church events. "The emphasis is on developing relationships as part of service, not just going to the site once and doing a service project and never seeing the people again," Campbell-Reed says.

Tips for Setting Boundaries
WITH CHILDREN AND YOUTH

Setting boundaries with children and youth means

● surrounding children and youth with caring adults and peers who model positive behaviors and who encourage them to be their best.

● setting and teaching clear rules and regulations for what is "in bounds" and what is "out of bounds" for behavior.

● stating, clarifying, and enforcing the consequences for breaking the rules.

When you're trying to build the boundaries-and-expectations assets, remember:

☐ **Start with yourself.** Are you self-disciplined? Do you set boundaries for yourself? Do you have high expectations for yourself? If you answered "no," then how can you become more intentional about your own boundaries and expectations?

☐ **Balance boundaries with support and love.** Boundaries and expectations work best when they're part of a caring relationship. When boundaries are enforced without a sense of love and support, they become punishment that alienates.

☐ **Think of discipline as teaching, not punishment.** Remember that discipline comes from the word "disciple." Use boundaries as tools for guiding and teaching young people to make good choices.

☐ **Talk about boundaries *before* you face the issue.** Don't wait until a problem has come up to set boundaries or to talk about expectations. Do it in advance—before the problems surface and escalate.

☐ **Give clear, specific messages.** Use language that's suitable to the child's age. Be specific about what you expect—and the consequences for not staying within the boundaries. Work with older children and teenagers to set mutually acceptable boundaries.

☐ **Set consequences that fit the misdeed.** Logical, natural consequences are best, when possible.

☐ **Reinforce in-bounds behaviors.** Affirm young people when they follow the boundaries. Let them know that you appreciate their positive choices. Tell them why.

☐ **Be forgiving.** It's important to set, monitor, and enforce boundaries. It's just as important that young people also learn about forgiveness. When the consequences have been applied, forgive, and move on.

Ideal Congregational Boundaries
AND EXPECTATIONS

Imagine yourself as the one who makes all the final decisions about boundaries and expectations at your church. Write one thing that you think would be a fair and clear expectation for each of the areas listed.

Worship attendance:

_____

_____

Christian education attendance:

_____

_____

Learning about your faith tradition:

_____

_____

Learning about teaching from the Bible:

_____

_____

Creating a warm Christian community:

_____

_____

Dealing with conflict within the congregation:

_____

_____

Supporting families with children and youth:

_____

_____

Involving children and youth in congregational decision making:

_____

_____

Helping people feel that others in the congregation care about them:

_____

_____

Ideas for Family Ministry to Set Boundaries and Expectations

- Create ways for families to get to know other families so that positive friendships can form.

- Provide parent education classes on child development so parents can learn what's reasonable to expect of their children at different ages.

- Talk with parents about their standards and boundaries for their children's conduct. Applaud their efforts when they have age-appropriate boundaries. When they don't, offer some practical alternatives.

- Provide opportunities for parents and teenagers to learn about and set boundaries and expectations together.

- Have a family ministry program on role models. Have family members identify their role models and discuss why they like them with other members of their family.

Ideas for Christian Education to Set Boundaries and Expectations

- Post rules in all Christian education rooms. Be clear about the consequences children can expect.

- Get parents' signed permission to publish a class roster with the children's names, addresses, phone numbers, and parents' names. This encourages relationships to form outside of the congregation as well as within the classroom.

- Have children survey (with adult supervision) neighbors who live near the church about any concerns they may have about behavior of church members. Find out what they expect and what they like.

- Encourage all adults within Christian education (including custodians and bus drivers) to be role models for children and youth.

- If at all possible, create boundaries of personal space for each young person, such as a desk, a cubby, and a hook to hang a coat on. Talk about the importance of personal spaces and encourage young people to respect each other's space and possessions.

Ideas for Intergenerational Ministry to Set Boundaries and Expectations

- Set and communicate clear policies about how everyone in the congregation is expected to treat the facilities and the consequences for not respecting those policies.

- Create mentoring and buddy programs in your congregation.

- Teach adults skills in setting boundaries so they're more comfortable talking to young people when a boundary is crossed.

- Plan intergenerational events with specific activities that encourage children and adults to mix so that young people can get to know their adult role models.

- Expect everyone of all ages to excel. Encourage parents to expect their children to do their best at school. Set high expectations for everyone in the congregation.

Ideas for Community Outreach to Set Boundaries and Expectations

- Equip congregational members to clarify boundaries for children and youth in their neighborhoods.

- Get involved in your community's efforts to limit young people's access to alcohol, tobacco, and other drugs.

- Establish and enforce clear ground rules for activities for community young people.

- Work with community young people to develop a statement of expectations for all children and youth in the community. Then sponsor conversations among young people and others about these expectations.

- Get involved in community planning. Encourage the group to use the asset framework in setting community policies, funding, and goals.

NOTES

1. L. Steinberg, B. Brown, and S.M. Dornbusch, *Beyond the Classroom: Why School Reform Has Failed and What Parents Need to Do* (New York: Simon and Schuster, 1996).

2. K.L. Kumpfer and C.W. Turner, "The Social Ecology Model of Adolescent Substance Abuse: Implications for Prevention," Special Issue: Preventive Interventions for Children at Risk, International Journal of the Addictions 25 (1990/1991): 435-463.

3. R.J. Sampson, S.W. Raudenbush, and F. Earls, "Neighborhoods and Violent Crime: A Multilevel Study of Collective Efficacy," Science 277 (1997) 918-924.

4. Peter L. Benson, Peter C. Scales, Nancy Leffert, and Eugene C. Roehlkepartain, *A Fragile Foundation: The State of Developmental Assets Among American Youth* (Minneapolis: Search Institute, 1999), 144.

5. Nancy Leffert, Peter L. Benson, and Jolene L. Roehlkepartain, *Starting Out Right: Developmental Assets for Children* (Minneapolis: Search Institute, 1997), 45.

6. Celia A. Brownell and Ernestine Brown, "Peers and Play in Infants and Toddlers," in Vincent B. Van Hasselt and Michel Hersen, eds., *Handbook of Social Development: A Lifespan Perspective*, (New York: Plenum, 1992), 183-200.

7. K.A. Urberg, S. Shyu, and J. Liang, "Peer Influence in Adolescent Cigarette Smoking," Addictive Behaviors 15 (1990): 247-255.

8. Peter C. Scales and Nancy Leffert, *Developmental Assets: A Synthesis of the Scientific Research on Adolescent Development* (Minneapolis: Search Institute, 1999), 90.

9. Eugene C. Roehlkepartain, "The Thinking Climate: A Missing Ingredient in Youth Ministry?" Christian Education Journal (Fall 1994).

10. Eugene C. Roehlkepartain and Peter L. Benson, *Youth in Protestant Churches: A Special Search Institute Report* (Minneapolis: Search Institute, 1993), 58.

Creating Meaningful Activities

Providing children and teenagers with opportunities to grow through programs and activities is an important way to help them grow up to be caring and competent. Participation in activities such as the arts, sports, and church groups has always been important, but it takes on even more significance in a time when so many young people are home alone after school and when everyday relationships across generations in extended families are less common.

Such opportunities for growth in constructive activities not only keep children and youth from getting bored (and in trouble), they also become the context in which young people build caring relationships with peers and adults, learn positive values, develop skills and competencies, and find opportunities for leadership and service. These activities can occur in many settings, from cocurricular activities in schools to clubs to creative arts and music activities to congregational programs for children and youth.

Many young people today do not participate in these positive activities. Search Institute research has found that only 54 percent of all young people spend six or more

hours per week in clubs, teams, or organizations in schools, youth programs, or churches.[1] Access is lowest among low-income, urban youth. A report from the National Commission on Children found that only 52 percent of low-income urban young people had access to clubs and organizations compared to 77 percent of low-income, nonurban young people.[2]

The need for positive activities must also be balanced with the reality of busyness in the lives of many children and youth, particularly those in suburban and middle or upper class communities. Young people need positive time alone and with their families (asset #20),

relaxing, reconnecting, and doing other things that are important for growing up.

Congregations clearly have an important role to play in providing structured, positive, and enriching activities for children and youth. These may include traditional activities such as Christian education, youth groups, music, and worship; or they may extend to an array of after-school and summer programs, athletic leagues, academic enrichment, and service opportunities.

There is also another important message for congregations in the constructive use of time assets: Young people need time at home. They need time to be by themselves. Thus, over-programming in ways that take young people away from home several evenings each week can interfere with young people's need for balance and varied opportunities for involvement.

ASSET #17:

Creative Activities

Early and ongoing exposure to the arts—music, drama, painting, for example—can have a profound effect on children and youth. Not only do young people who participate in the arts develop an appreciation for aesthetics, but they also learn skills, build discipline (by practicing on a regular basis), develop self-expression, and enhance their self-esteem.

Creative activities can begin at birth. Even infants respond to music. Newborns increase their sucking when they hear folk music. Babies between the ages of four and six months even begin to bounce to the beat of music. Researchers say that daily experiences in the arts not only add pleasure to a child's life, but also predict higher test scores in fourth and fifth grade.[3]

Teenagers also greatly benefit from creative activities. Researchers have found that young people who are involved in creative activities tend to have a higher self-esteem, have more creativity, be more self-motivated, have long-term retention, and higher achievement.[4]

Children's choirs and youth choirs are often hallmarks of many churches. Arts and crafts also are often emphasized. But many churches can do more with creative activities. Children and youth can put on an annual play or an annual musical for the congregation. Young people can paint or do other artistic projects that can then be displayed in classrooms, hallways, and church entrances. Children and teenagers can play solos, duets, and trios during the worship service as they learn new instruments from piano to guitar to violin.

Creative activities is the least reported of all the forty assets. Search Institute researchers have found that 19 percent of all young people have this asset and that there's a wide gap between guys and girls. While 24 percent of girls report having this asset, only 14 percent of boys do. By the twelfth grade, the percentages have fallen even more with 18 percent of girls and 13 percent of guys saying they have asset #17: creative activities.

ASSET #18:

Child and Youth Programs

Child and youth programs cover a rich territory of clubs, teams, and organizations. These can include congregationally based programs (such as Bible studies and children's programs), school-based and after-school activities, community-based programs, local affiliates of national organizations (such as Camp Fire, Girl Scouts, Boy Scouts, Boys and Girls Clubs, 4-H Clubs, YWCA, YMCA, and Junior Achievement) and parachurch groups (such as Young Life, Fellowship of Christian Athletes, Boys' and Girls' Brigade, Youth for Christ, and Pioneer Clubs).

Activities outside the home provide children and teenagers with opportunities to discover the world around them and to figure out their place in the world. Programs are places of exploration, discovery, and learning. Infants need stimulating out-of-home activities such as going to the grocery store, to a concert in the park, for a walk at the zoo. Older children need supervised, structured activities that allow them to interact with children outside the home and that encourage them to grow and learn new skills.

In short, involvement in constructive programs and activities away from school and home can have many benefits, including

- connecting children and youth to principled and caring adults.

- nurturing young people's skills and capacities through group activities, lessons, relationships, and supervision.

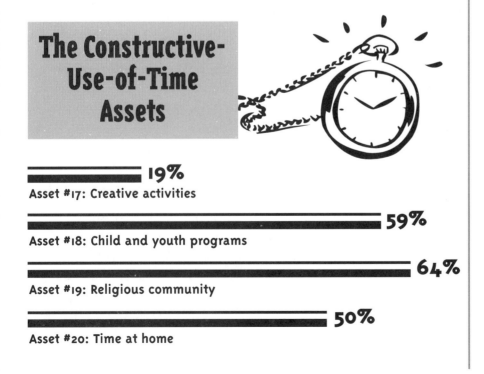

The Constructive-Use-of-Time Assets

19%
Asset #17: Creative activities

59%
Asset #18: Child and youth programs

64%
Asset #19: Religious community

50%
Asset #20: Time at home

AN ASSET-BUILDING CONGREGATION

Providing Constructive Activities

Members of First United Methodist Church in Albuquerque, New Mexico, didn't have to look hard to uncover the needs of youth in the community. A look out the window easily revealed the need for after-school activities for youth and a safe place for them to go. In cooperation with the schools, the congregation developed a variety of after-school activities to help build developmental assets in the youth in their congregation as well as in the community. Having been introduced to the asset-building framework, they knew the importance of intergenerational relationships and tried to integrate that element as much as possible.

Every Monday afternoon the church opens its doors to youth from the local middle school for recreation, help with homework, and movies. Soon the congregation will launch their own publishing company called Longfellow. Elementary school children will write, illustrate, and bind their own books. The congregation also plans to start a bicycle club where kids can learn basic bike repair.

- protecting youth from violence and other dangerous or negative influences.
- creating a peer group that exerts positive influence on young people.
- providing opportunities for young people to contribute to their congregation, community, and society through service and leadership.

Programs and clubs are an important way to empower young people.[5] Researchers have found that if adult leaders are knowledgeable and well-trained, they allow children and youth to make or assist in decisions about activities. Especially with groups for teenagers, clubs can establish a partnership of shared responsibility between the teenagers and the adults.

Congregations can provide programs that not only nurture young people's spirituality but build their skills and cement relationships with other young people. Children's ministry programs, youth groups, confirmation classes, young people's Bible study, a church softball team, and specific Christian clubs can all build this asset.

Search Institute researchers have found that 59 percent of all young people say they have this asset, with both guys and girls reporting essentially the same levels of involvement.

Religious Community

Involvement in a church promotes positive development because it exposes children and youth to positive values and to positive relationship-building activities. Churches are one of the few places that intentionally address moral development, which is an integral part of healthy development. Studies of families involved in congregations consistently find that the parent's religious values are strong predictors of the child's moral and religious values.[6]

Churches also are one of the few remaining intergenerational communities to which children and youth have access. In fact, with the high mobility of Americans today, some children and teenagers rarely see their grandparents and other extended family. A church gives young people a chance to connect with people of other ages, and churches that are intentional about building intergenerational community build assets in young people. In addition, churches are also one of the few places where long-term intergenerational relationships can be formed. For example, one Sunday school teacher decided to keep moving up a grade each year to continue building the relationships with young people.

Churches also have the opportunity to provide a wide variety of structured activities for children and teenagers. Weekly educational classes, youth groups, children's ministry events, service projects, and mission trips not only enhance this asset but other assets as well, such as asset #18: child and youth programs and

#9: service to others.

Researchers have found that young people who spend time in a church have an increased sense of well-being, an increased self-esteem, and increased life satisfaction. Church involvement also appears to decrease problems, too. Young people who are part of a church community are less likely to use alcohol, marijuana, and other drugs. They're also less likely to get involved in sexual activity at an early age, and they have lower levels of depression.[7]

Search Institute researchers have found that 64 percent of all young people are involved in a religious community. Girls are more likely to report having this asset (68 percent) than guys (61 percent). The biggest difference occurs in tenth grade when 67 percent of girls report having this asset compared to 57 percent of guys.

There is also a major difference in this asset based on age. Almost three-fourths of sixth graders surveyed (72 percent) say they spend at least one hour per week in religious activities. Involvement drops to 54 percent among twelfth-graders.

Many people comment on the high percentages of this asset compared to involvement in other activities. A reason for this difference is that the other constructive-use-of-time assets have *three* hours per week as the standard. Asset #19: religious community sets the level at *one* hour per week (only minimal regular religious involvement). Only 19 percent of the young people surveyed participate in religious activities three or more hours per week. Thus young people, on average, actually spend less time in religious activities than other youth programs.

AN ASSET-BUILDING CHURCH

Music Lessons

First Presbyterian Church in downtown Knoxville, Tennessee, became a community arts school during its under-utilized daytime hours. The church set out to provide music lessons for children and youth who otherwise would be unable to afford them.

Margaret Bell, who helped start the program, recruited volunteers from both within and outside the congregation to develop the program. They raised funds for teachers and musical instruments from the Junior League, Knoxville Parks and Recreation Department, Knoxville Arts Alliance, Knoxville Housing Authority, and other sources.

Today about forty young people receive music lessons from the church. In addition to getting lessons, each young person is paired with an adult artist/mentor from the community.

"I could tell you story upon story about what the [music lessons] have done for kids' lives," Bell says. She mentioned "positive relationships, improved self-esteem, and better grades—in addition to the joy of making music."

ASSET #20:

Time at Home

Although children and teenagers tend to spend too much time *alone* at home (often just accompanied by the television), it's developmentally important that they spend time at home with their parents and siblings. The activities that families share—hanging out together, cooking and eating together, doing homework, doing chores, playing together, talking together—are the activities that help young people grow up healthy. In too many communities, young people spend virtually every evening away from home either doing structured activities or hanging out with friends.

Although the three other constructive-use-of-time assets can easily pull young people away from home, this final constructive use of time asset calls for a sense of balance and a sense of family togetherness. "Neither children nor adults should be expected to function at the utmost limits of their capacities every day, all day," says Lillian G. Katz, professor of early childhood education at the University of Illinois at Urbana-Champaign. "We are all more likely to do well when there is a balance between our tasks and activities."[8]

Some churches have designated family-at-home nights on their calendars and have ensured that no meetings or other events are scheduled. Others have been intentional about coordinating events on a single night so that the entire family can come to church, eat dinner together, and then go to separate activities, such as a church choir practice, meetings, or a children's activity. All of these things are ways to promote asset #20: time at home.

Search Institute researchers have found that 50 percent of all young people say they spend two or fewer nights per week out with friends "with nothing special to do," which is how the time-at-home asset is measured. There is little difference in the level of this asset when comparing guys and girls. However, this asset declines from 55 percent of sixth-graders to 39 percent of twelfth-graders.

Ideas for All Ministries to Create Meaningful Activities

- If you offer midweek children's and family activities, coordinate with other congregations in your community to designate a specific night of the week to schedule family congregational activities. Then work with schools and organized sports teams not to schedule activities on that night. For example, some communities choose Wednesday night.

- Plan activities for children and teenagers during the summer, even if attendance is lower. Talk with parents to identify needs and interests of their children.

- Find out what hinders family attendance. For example, in some communities, families find themselves having to choose between an organized sports game and a worship service. A group of congregations worked

with the Boston City Parks and Recreation Department to help raise money for outdoor lighting. The new lighting allowed games to be scheduled at night and helped many families who were trying to chose between morning worship services and ballgames.

- Teach children and youth some songs from your faith tradition. Incorporate actions and humor to make singing more fun.

- Create an "active noisy room" for parents with young children to go to during worship services if infants cry or toddlers become restless. This room can be far away from the sanctuary; however, wire it with speakers so parents can still listen to the service.

Ideas for Church Nurseries to Create Meaningful Activities

- Incorporate creative activities with infants and toddlers in your church nursery. Give young children new paintbrushes and watercolors, and encourage them to paint on "outdoor canvases" like sidewalks or walls.

- Once or twice a year plan a nursery program for families to attend. Play a few icebreakers, then demonstrate some of the activities you do with the children in your care. Allow time for families to mingle and get to know each other.

- Use a cassette or CD player to play singalong music and also lullabies for nap time.

- Create a list of fun ideas that families can do together at home.

Make copies of this list and distribute them to parents.

- Invite a musician to visit your church nursery to play some music. Often a community band or community orchestra has people willing to do this.

Ideas for Children's Ministry to Create Meaningful Activities

- Start a children's choir that sings in worship about four times a year. (It's difficult for children to come to weekly rehearsals. Instead have one or two rehearsals before each concert, or set aside ten to fifteen minutes during the Christian education hour to practice.)

- Survey your congregation to find the artists and musicians who would be willing to come to a children's ministry activity once. For example, children can follow a flutist who leads them for a walk around the church building, or a craftsperson can show them a simple art project that uses colorful buttons.

- Encourage members who are musicians and other artists to offer free lessons to young people who can't afford private lessons.

- Create meaningful programs that build skills in children. For example, you could have a church astronomy group that meets one evening to look at the stars. Help children identify certain constellations in the sky. A program doesn't have to be ongoing. Sometimes you can create a worthwhile program that just meets once.

- Encourage other children and youth programs to use church space during under-utilized times of the day. For example, a Girl or Boy Scout troop could meet in your church building. Give children a tour of your church facility. Explore places that they might not be familiar with.

- Talk about animals that appear in Bible stories and encourage children to make the sounds of these animals.

- Encourage children's workers to spend a little one-on-one time with each child during an activity. Ask adults to get down on the child's level (by squatting down or sitting next to the child) and ask the child a few questions about their interests and hobbies. This can make the child feel special and help the child want to come back to church.

Ideas for Youth Ministry to Create Meaningful Activities

- Provide enriching after-school activities for young people. Encourage members of the congregation to volunteer to share their hobbies and interests with youth.

- Plan summer service projects, mission projects, and workcamps far in advance so teenagers can get those dates on the calendar ahead of time. Make a big deal about these activities so teenagers know they're worthwhile.

- Work with young people's schedules, not against them. Some youth groups meet before school for breakfast since so many young people have part-time jobs

and extracurricular activities.

- Coordinate church youth activities with school calendars so young people aren't away from home too many nights of the week.

- Encourage young people to be involved in music, art, and drama. Attend their concerts and performances and show them your support.

Ideas for Family Ministry to Create Meaningful Activities

- Respect limits on involvement and make the time parents are involved enriching, giving back to the family more than is taken away.

- Sponsor after-school programs for children and teenagers of working parents.

- Create an activity in which families can evaluate their family life. Encourage families to honestly evaluate how much they enjoy being with each other. Give lots of ideas on how families can share more enjoyable times together at home.

- Remember that families are busy. Respect their time by starting and ending family ministry events on time.

- Create meaningful church activities that families can do together. Some churches create an annual family choir. Others have an annual family play in which children, teenagers, and adults are involved in performances. Some have an annual event in which children and parents make decorations for the church's

AN ASSET-BUILDING ECUMENICAL COMMUNITY

A Worthwhile Activity

Every year several congregations in Albuquerque, New Mexico, join together to provide a safe New Year's Eve celebration for area young people. The teenagers travel on buses to a concert, a worship service, ice skating, dancing, and in-line skating; then wind it up with a late-late-late movie at 5:30 in the morning. Adults from participating congregations provide supervision for the event. Youth worker Toni McNeill is part of the New Year's Eve committee. "We want our kids to see there is a good way to have fun, and it doesn't have to be trouble," she says. "And we're really excited that this interfaith event keeps growing. Our goal to is make it the 'in thing' for youth to do in Albuquerque on New Year's Eve!"

Christmas tree and decorate it on the first day of Advent.

Ideas for Christian Education to Create Meaningful Activities

- Integrate the arts into Christian education lessons. Have students make up a song about the Exodus or create a relief map of the Holy Land using clay.

- Be creative in your teaching. For example, when children are learning about Jesus calling the fishermen, take the children fishing at a nearby lake.

- Ask children whether the crafts you use in Christian education classes are interesting. If not, research more creative ideas.

- Have an annual family Christian education lesson and invite the parents and siblings of children to your classroom. Create a list of ideas that families can do together at home to nurture their faith and have enjoyable times together as a family.

- Invite adults who lead programs for children and young people to speak with your class. Have them talk about the programs they lead and encourage young people to get involved.

Ideas for Intergenerational Ministry to Create Meaningful Activities

- When planning activities for the whole congregation, be sure that you keep in mind the needs of young people who will participate.

- Have a music-swapping event where each person brings their favorite song and gets to share it with the group.

- Form intergenerational music groups (bands, choirs, or orchestras) and ask them to lead in worship and other occasions from time to time.

- Encourage people from all generations to participate in sports and recreational activities, such as church softball and basketball leagues.

- Plan challenging, fun intergenerational activities, such as hosting a church square dance, painting a church mural on a hallway wall, or setting up "puzzle fun," in which puzzles of varying difficulty can be put together.

- Create a video story (or history) of your church. Have children and youth interview older members and include clips from various intergenerational activities.

Ideas for Community Outreach to Create Meaningful Activities

- Sponsor free events at your church to expose young people to stimulating artistic expression, such as African drumming, flamenco dancing, and yodeling.

- Sponsor or cosponsor after-school care for community children and youth. Provide recreational activities, study space, tutoring, or computer training.

- Encourage church members to be coaches, sponsors, mentors, or leaders in community sports, recreational, and other youth programs in the community and schools. Consider their community involvement part of your church's ministry in the community.

- Cosponsor a hotline with other congregations and organizations so young people can call to learn about available programs and activities.

- Advocate public support for child and youth programs in schools, parks, and community centers.

- Cosponsor a youth drop-in center with other congregations and organizations. If your congregation has a large facility, make it available for this purpose.

NOTES

1. Search Institute, "Five Fundamental Resources for Children and Youth" (Alexandria, VA: America's Promise— The Alliance for Youth, 1997).

2. National Commission on Children, *Speaking of Kids: A National Survey of Children and Parents* (Washington, DC: National Commission on Children, 1991).

3. Robert H. Bradley, Bettye M. Caldwell, and Stephen L. Rock, "Home Environment and School Performance: A Ten-Year Follow-Up Examination of Three Models of Environmental Action," Child Development 59 (1988): 852-867.

4. Peter C. Scales and Nancy Leffert, *Developmental Assets: A Synthesis of the Scientific Research on Adolescent Development* (Minneapolis: Search Institute, 1999), 100.

5. J.S. Dubas, and B.A. Snider, "The Role of Community-Based Youth Groups in Enhancing Learning and Achievement Through Nonformal Education," in R.M. Lerner, ed., *Early Adolescence: Perspectives on Research, Policy, and Intervention* (Hillsdale, NJ: Lawrence Erlbaum, 1993), 159-174.

6. Bradley R. Hertel and Michael Hughes, "Religious Affiliation, Attendance, and Support for 'Pro-Family' Issues in the United States," Social Forces 65 (1987): 858-882.

7. Peter C. Scales and Nancy Leffert, *Developmental Assets: A Synthesis of the Scientific Research on Adolescent Development* (Minneapolis: Search Institute, 1999), 102-103.

8. Lillian G. Katz, "Overloaded Kids," Parents 66, no. 3 (March 1991): 186.

Guidelines for Effective

FAMILY MINISTRY PROGRAMMING

In their book *Ministry to Families With Teenagers*, Dub Ambrose and Walt Mueller list sixteen guidelines for effective family programming:

☐ 1. Remember basic programming principles regarding preparation and engaging activities.

☐ 2. Focus on common family concerns, not just concerns of parents or of young people.

☐ 3. Be sensitive to different family situations.

☐ 4. Facilitate cooperation so families work together, not compete.

☐ 5. Let families communicate; don't just talk to them.

☐ 6. Begin with nonthreatening activities.

☐ 7. Don't let parents dominate.

☐ 8. Remember that parents are adults.

☐ 9. Avoid addressing just one generation.

☐ 10. Help each generation respect the other.

☐ 11. Be sensitive to participants without all family members present.

☐ 12. Keep costs down.

☐ 13. Recognize physical limitations.

☐ 14. Plan for other ages, such as younger children.

☐ 15. Include time for relaxing.

☐ 16. Use different leaders, both parents and young people.

Adapted from Dub Ambrose and Walt Mueller, *Ministry to Families With Teenagers* (Loveland, CO: Group, 1988), 85-94.

Involving Unconnected Young People

IN CONGREGATIONAL PROGRAMS

As you develop programs and activities, keep in mind a balance of activities that address the needs of young people who participate regularly as well as those in the community whom the congregation is reaching out to involve. For this last group, a key challenge is to provide a climate in which they feel comfortable and where they will not be embarrassed because they are unfamiliar with religious concepts, language, or traditions.

Here are six specific suggestions for helping visitors and unconnected young people feel welcome in your congregational programs:

☐ **1. Plan for visitors.** Always assume there will be visitors. Always have children and youth wear name tags. Provide music books, even for songs that "everyone knows."

☐ **2. Pay attention to visitors.** Encourage everyone in the group to pay attention and take time to talk with visitors and include them in conversations and activities. Too often regular attendees are busy catching up with their friends and leaving out the visitors.

☐ **3. Show visitors around.** Assign regular attendees to be guides for any visitors who come, showing them around your church and helping with specific traditions of your church.

☐ **4. Ask visitors what they want to do.** When newcomers express interest in becoming regulars, it can be tempting to get them involved in everything that is important to you. Instead, ask them what they're interested in doing. Then find opportunities within your congregation that fit those interests.

☐ **5. Give low-risk opportunities for involvement.** Evaluate your overall program to ensure that you have some relative low-risk entry points through which children and youth can get involved at their own pace.

☐ **6. Follow up with visitors.** When a young person visits, have someone (preferably a young person) follow up to answer questions and invite the visitor to future activities. If someone attends several activities and then stops, check to be sure everything is OK.

What Activities Does Your Church

Many different types of programs can help to build the constructive-use-of-time assets. This chart lists several broad categories of programming for children, youth, and families. In each one, note the specific kinds of programs and activities your church sponsors. Then note the strengths and challenges for each activity, based on your understanding of developmental assets.

CATEGORY	PROGRAM NAME	ASSET-BUILDING STRENGTHS	ASSET-BUILDING CHALLENGES
Christian education			
Music, drama, and other arts			
Sports and recreation			
Service and leadership			

Offer Children, Youth, & Families?

CATEGORY	PROGRAM NAME	ASSET-BUILDING STRENGTHS	ASSET-BUILDING CHALLENGES
Small group activities			
Social activities			
Retreats and trips			
Other			

Emphasizing a Commitment

Curiosity, the ability to internalize new knowledge, and the discipline required by learning are all important to healthy development. The ability to connect school with other aspects of life is vital in our ever-changing society.

This kind of commitment can be nurtured in all children and youth, not just those who are good in school. Sometimes it begins when someone focuses attention on helping young people discover the joy of learning. And it's the kind of commitment we seek to instill in children and teenagers in our congregations so that they—and we—continue to study, grow, and learn.

The commitment-to-learning assets address both current educational commitments as well as young people's long-term aspirations. They also draw attention to the informal learning that occurs when young people read for pleasure.

Commitment to learning is the category of assets that Christian leaders sometimes have the most trouble connecting to their own priorities (unless their congregation sponsors a parochial school or other formal educational endeavor).

However, there are clear connections between the commitment-to-learning assets and some basic tasks in spiritual growth and formation. For example, we want young people to be motivated to learn the basics of Christian faith, beliefs, and life. We want them to be actively engaged in learning as part of Christian education programs. Thus, while the specific ways Search Institute's forty assets are defined and measured may be relevant for churches only to the extent that they reinforce school-based learning, the principles and goals that underlie each asset are critical for effectively teaching and nurturing faith and discipleship.

In addition, there are a number of places where many churches can and already do address formal learning. These include:

● developing computer labs for young people and their parents.

● offering space for young people to study after school with congregational members volunteering as tutors.

● affirming young people's educational commitments through recognition for academic achievement.

● respecting students' study needs in scheduling activities.

● supporting parents in playing an active role in their children's education.

● sponsoring or supporting private schools as an integral part of the church's mission and ministry.

ASSET #21:

Achievement Motivation

The motivation to achieve is related to a young person taking pride in her or his own ability and feeling a sense of self-fulfillment. Researcher Susan Harter found that children tend to strive to achieve either to satisfy their own needs (intrinsic motivation) or to earn incentives, such as grades and rewards (extrinsic motivation). Intrinsically motivated children prefer challenging tasks and see themselves as more competent compared to children who are motivated extrinsically.

Children who are intrinsically motivated also are more likely to develop self-initiative that enhances their growth in all areas of life, whether they are playing, doing homework, or learning a new skill.[1]

In congregations we want young people to desire to do well in their Christian education classes. We want them to achieve in learning about their faith, their spiritual heritage, and stories from Scripture. In its national study on Protestant congregations, Search Institute researchers found that effective Christian education blends biblical knowledge and insight with major issues that the age group faces. For teenagers these issues include sexuality, chemical use, and friendship.[2] Creating a stimulating Christian education environment is more conducive to motivating young people to learn.

Search Institute researchers found that 63 percent of all young people report having asset #21: achievement motivation. Girls are much more likely than guys to say they have this asset. While 71 percent of girls report having this asset, only 56 percent of guys do.

ASSET #22:

School Engagement

Being engaged and attentive is another way to have a commitment to learning. Adults who are responsive and attentive can set the stage for children and teenagers to become engaged in learning. When children see their parents and other adults fully involved in their work, school, community, and home, they learn that becoming absorbed in an activity is important.

Researchers have found that young people who are engaged in school (or in play as young children) are

- less likely to use drugs.
- less likely to get pregnant by age nineteen.
- more likely to get absorbed in their studies.
- more likely to spend more time on homework.
- more likely to attend college.
- have better school attendance.
- feel more supported at school and at home.[3]

Young people who are engaged in learning are easy to find. They're the children who get excited about Solomon's Temple and spend hours studying it. They're the teenagers who map out all the places Paul traveled, or the young people who act on their faith and serve others. They become excited and absorbed in what they're doing.

Search Institute researchers have found that 64 percent of all young people report having asset #22: school engagement. Girls are more likely than guys to report having this asset. While 71 percent of girls says they have this asset, only 56 percent of guys do.

ASSET #23:

Homework

Children and teenagers who do homework are more likely to grow up to be motivated, responsible adults.[4] Parents can support this asset by helping a child set up a homework area, developing a homework

The Commitment-to-Learning Assets

63%

Asset #21: Achievement motivation

64%

Asset #22: School engagement

45%

Asset #23: Homework

51%

Asset #24: Bonding to school

24%

Asset #25: Reading for pleasure

AN ASSET-BUILDING CHURCH

A Premier Preschool

Although churches and adults say they value education, often education suffers because no one is willing to invest time and money in it. Yet Our Saviour Lutheran Church in Bremerton, Washington, received honors for having one of the top ten preschools in the country.

Staff pay was a key factor for Sycamore Tree Preschool, the ministry of the church, for receiving the award. "Our teachers earn $14 an hour, but it should be $20," says Jocelyn Bright, who recently retired as Sycamore's director. The median pay for a preschool teacher is $7.80 an hour.

Because Sycamore pays more, there is less staff turnover. Four of the preschool's staff members have been with the preschool for ten years or more. All have degrees or certificates in early childhood education.

Although the congregation pays higher salaries to staff, it doesn't charge higher fees for parents. Sycamore charges $105 a month for the pre-kindergarten class that meets three days a week for two and half hours. A similar program in Chicago costs $155.

"The preschool is one of the most important local ministries supported by the congregation," Bright says. "It tells the community that this church cares about children and their future."

routine, and assisting with assignments when the child needs help. Churches can set up homework help lines, tutoring, and places to study after school. Teachers in Christian education can assign homework designed to enrich learning, not just to give children something they have to do.

When asset #23 pertains to infants, toddlers, and preschoolers, Search Institute researchers refer to it as stimulating activity. Many researchers have found that the amount and quality of stimulation in children's early home and care-giving environments, such as child-care centers, preschools, and church nurseries, will affect later achievement and even IQ scores.[5] Parental involvement in play (such as the parent interacting and structuring play periods with the child) and high-quality play materials (such as age-appropriate toys) during infancy and preschool are strong predictors of achievement in the fourth and fifth grades.[6]

Church nurseries, Christian education classes, confirmation classes, and Bible studies all are ideal settings for building this asset. In church nurseries, volunteers who encourage children to explore and provide stimulating toys that match each child's emerging skills (such as crawling, pulling up, or walking, for example) build the foundation for this asset. Christian education classes and confirmation classes can assign meaningful homework that challenges young people intellectually and spiritually.

Overall, 45 percent of all young people report having asset #23: homework. Search Institute researchers found that girls are more

Characteristics of Effective Christian

I n a major study of eleven thousand youth and adults in congregations in six Protestant denominations, Search Institute identified qualities of Christian education programs that help nurture a strong, mature faith.[7] People are more likely to grow in their faith if their church's Christian education has the following:

Educational approaches that...

☐ emphasize connecting the Bible and faith to life issues, including friendships, sexuality, decision making, and world issues.

☐ create a sense of community in which each person is challenged to think independently and to apply faith to life.

☐ emphasize intergenerational contact and service to others.

A coordinated plan that...

☐ engages people of all ages in studying the same material simultaneously.

☐ assesses needs, sets goals and learning objectives, and evaluates programs, teachers, and other leaders.

☐ provides opportunities for teachers to plan, learn, and grow.

Teachers who...

☐ are high in faith maturity.

☐ know educational theory and practice for their age group.

☐ care about their students.

Congregational leadership that includes...

☐ a pastor who is committed to, knowledgeable of, and involved in Christian education for all ages.

☐ a governing board that regularly addresses Christian education.

AN ADULT IN ASSET-BUILDING ACTION

Dr. Kent Gulden

Kent Gulden, DDS, builds assets through his Bikes for Books contest that is held three times a year. The White Bear Lake, Minnesota, orthodontist, has been encouraging children ages six to thirteen to read for the past three years through the contests that he sponsors at his practice, the elementary school, a congregation, and the community library.

Children who participate in the contest read books, write the title and author of each book, and provide a twenty-five-word description about the book. All the readers names are put into a drawing, and children draw the names of three winners. Each winner receives a three-hundred-dollar gift certificate from a local business that sells bicycles, skis, and other recreational equipment.

Children who don't win start reading again to see if they can win in the next contest. In addition, Dr. Gulden displays artwork of fourth graders from a nearby elementary school during American Education Week. Artwork covers the lobby and all the walls of his office. On another wall, the orthodontist posts all the letters and pictures that children send him.

likely than guys to have this asset. While 53 percent of girls say they have this asset, only 37 percent of guys say they do. By twelfth grade, only 31 percent of guys report having this asset.

ASSET #24:

Bonding to School

When children and youth go to school, their interest in learning helps them bond to—or become invested in—school. Young people not only need to gain knowledge and skills in school, but researchers have found that bonding to school is a particularly important factor for promoting school success and academic achievement.[8] Too often, negative perceptions of schools and other learning institutions (such as libraries) by parents and other adults can inhibit young people's learning and reduce their learning opportunities. When churches focus all their attention on problems in schools, they can unintentionally interfere with this asset as young people internalize the message that schools are "bad places."

Congregations are also places of learning—children and youth may bond to their congregations when they enjoy learning and find what they're learning stimulating and challenging. In its research on Protestant congregations, Search Institute researchers found that effective Christian education programs are associated not only with greater faith maturity but also with greater loyalty to the congregation and denomination.[9] In other words, quality Christian education helps young people bond to their church. The "Characteristics of Effective Christian Edu-

cation Programs" box highlights key elements of effective Christian education programs.

Search Institute researchers found that 51 percent of all young people have asset #24: bonding to school. While 56 percent of girls say they have this asset, only 46 percent of guys do. A low point occurs during the eighth grade, when 40 percent of guys and 51 percent of girls say they have this asset.

ASSET #25:

Reading for Pleasure

Of the five commitment-to-learning assets, the one asset young people are least likely to have is asset #25: reading for pleasure. This asset is also one of the least reported assets among the forty assets. Yet, as the Commission on Reading says in its report *Becoming a Nation of Readers*, "Reading is a cornerstone for a child's success in school and indeed, throughout life."[10]

Reading to children, even from infancy, helps boost their skills. Researchers found that picture-book reading to young children was related to their understanding of what is being said. These children were more likely to develop oral language skills earlier, meaning they not only talked earlier but they also understood what other people were saying earlier than other children.[11] Reading also helps children adjust to new situations. One study found that children's literature that portrayed positive and negative aspects of school helped children deal with new situations in the classroom and relationships with their peers.[12]

However, young people's enthusiasm

for reading can easily wane as they get older. After-school activities, television, and friendships often compete (and win) against reading. Influencing and inspiring young people to read (rather than trying to control what they read) usually encourages young people to be lifelong readers. Some young people go through phases in which they read only comic books or magazines. Although adults may prefer that young people read books, it's more important for young people to be reading *something* than nothing at all.

While 24 percent of all young people report having asset #25: reading for pleasure, Search Institute researchers found a wide difference between guys and girls. While 30 percent of girls say they have this asset, only 19 percent of guys say they do. For guys, the ninth, tenth, and eleventh grades are low points: Only 17 percent of guys say they have this asset during these years.

Ideas for All Ministries to Instill a Commitment to Learning

- Emphasize the importance of lifelong learning by having stimulating learning opportunities for people of all ages.

- Make a congregational library (even if it's small). Stock it with books for children, youth, and adults. Encourage people to visit it often by featuring select titles in your congregational newsletter or bulletin on a regular basis.

- Encourage adults to model their enthusiasm for learning.

- Challenge more adults to teach, emphasizing how much they learn through teaching others.

- Encourage adults in the church to volunteer in schools, spending time reading or tutoring, sharing talents, or providing other leadership.

- Partner with schools to develop donation drives that benefit education. For example, a congregation can raise money so a school can add more books to its library.

- Celebrate and honor teachers who attend your church. Help them see their work as a ministry.

- Sponsor a congregational read-a-thon. Have people of all ages read books for one month.

Ideas for Church Nurseries to Instill a Commitment to Learning

- Make your nursery a warm, inviting place where parents are excited to bring children, which builds asset #24: enjoyment of learning. This builds loyalty to your nursery, which also builds loyalty to your congregation in general.

- Circulate types of toys in and out of storage so that you can introduce new toys to children often, while putting others away. This will keep your nursery staff from always feeling the need to buy more toys, and children will feel stimulated by the constant stream of new toys.

- Encourage congregational members to donate age-appropriate board books for the nursery.

- Recruit volunteers that are curious and motivated to learn.

Their attitudes rub off on children.

- Notice when an infant or toddler becomes engrossed in an activity. Nurture that child's interest by spending some one-on-one time with the child and the activity.

Ideas for Children's Ministry to Instill a Commitment to Learning

- Make reading part of your usual activities. Check out books from your community library or visit a used book store for bargains.

- Keep creating new small groups of children to do learning activities together. Since elementary-age children will begin to form tight groups with children from their school, be attuned to children who may feel left out, especially those who don't attend the same schools as the children in your church.

- Attend school performances, sporting events, plays, and concerts of the children in your ministry. Show support to the children you serve by being a presence in their school activities from time to time.

- Have activities that emphasize eating well and getting enough sleep so children begin to see the connection between taking care of themselves and feeling alert and ready to learn.

- Read aloud to children as a part of classes and activities. In addition to Bible stories, find children's books that reinforce the point of your lessons.

AN ASSET-BUILDING DENOMINATION

Instilling a Commitment to Learning

In 1997 the U.S. Department of Education launched the America Reads Challenge to ensure that all children can read well and independently by the end of third grade. The religious community was challenged to recruit volunteers for this effort, and many denominations quickly got involved. Here are some ways various denominations have supported literacy.

• The Presbyterian Church (U.S.A.) declared 1998 the "Year of Education" to focus congregations' attention on reading and tutoring.

• The Progressive National Baptist Convention focused on the challenge at its annual convention of fifteen thousand delegates.

• The United Methodist Church is publishing resources for churches to use in supporting education in their community.[13]

Ideas for Youth Ministry to Instill a Commitment to Learning

● Examine youth activities to ensure that they use educational processes that challenge and stimulate youth. Examine the topics covered to ensure that they're relevant to young people's lives.

● Sponsor a homework hot line or places to study after school for young people who can benefit from more structure.

● Make reading a regular part of youth activities. If some young people struggle with reading and are interested in some extra help, find congregation members who are willing to tutor.

● Encourage teenagers to talk about the schools they attend. Have teenagers compare schools, since many congregations have young people who attend a variety of schools.

● Develop opportunities for teenagers to link up with adults who share their academic interests. For example, have an adult who enjoys literature lead a book study group for teenagers. Or have an adult who enjoys geology take teenagers out rock hunting.

● Make service and mission trips educational. Debrief experiences and tie in Scripture and learning.

● Incorporate a wide variety of learning activities, including ones that get young people to move and use their five senses.

● Encourage church members and staff to attend youth activities at school as a sign of support and to help build asset #24: bonding to school.

● Talk with young people about their educational plans. Encourage them to stretch themselves.

Ideas for Family Ministry to Instill a Commitment to Learning

● Sponsor small groups of parents who might study a book, watch a video, or have another form of ongoing, peer-led discussion.

● Alert parents to parent educational opportunities in the community. Have parents sign up, go as a group, then discuss the topic in a follow-up conversation.

● Encourage families to support their schools and show school spirit. In the fall, for example, encourage families to wear their school colors to a family ministry gathering that revolves around the importance of school.

● Offer parent and teenager workshops on asset-building topics, such as positive family communication (asset #2) and effective decision making. (asset #32).

● Create parent-child book groups. Have a mother-daughter book group and a father-son book group to read books together and discuss them afterward.

Ideas for Christian Education to Instill a Commitment to Learning

● Create an atmosphere of discovery, challenge, and learning in all classrooms. Learn how to make learning more engaging, interesting, and challenging.

● Make a wish list of toys, supplies, and educational items you would like in your classroom. Post these lists outside your classroom and in the church newsletter. Parents and others adults may be able to make some of your wishes come true.

● Talk about the ups and downs of learning. Sometimes learning is hard, sometimes easy. Help children find ways to stay involved in learning when they start feeling bored.

● Create learning activities that stretch young people in terms of their thinking and creativity.

● Since your classrooms may have young people from many different schools, encourage young people to talk about their school environments.

● Give each young person a turn at reading a book aloud to an entire class. For young children who aren't reading yet, have them show a picture book and tell a story based on what they see. Teenagers often enjoy reading books to younger children.

● Be enthusiastic about what you're teaching. One teacher created monthly topics for the class to learn about in depth. She talked about how each month the topic was more interesting to her than the topic before. (She put these topics in order of least interesting to her to most interesting.) She kept building to her favorite topic, which the class studied during May. Topics for first graders might include penguins, rain forests, and whales (and how God made all these wonderful animals and plants). The teacher ended with whales, excitedly telling about her whale-watching expeditions.

Ideas for Intergenerational Ministry to Instill a Commitment to Learning

● Publicly celebrate young people's progress and milestones in school.

● Encourage adult members to attend the school activities of children and young people in your church.

● Celebrate when children and youth are honored at school for their accomplishments. Announce their honors during worship services or in newsletters.

● Support local schools by announcing upcoming music, drama, sports, and other school events in the congregational newsletter.

● Invite young people and adults to bring beach towels or blankets to your church. Once it gets dark, have everyone lie outside to look at the stars in the sky. Name constellations. Count stars!

● Form plant partners. Have an intergenerational event to study plants. Encourage people to bring in their favorite plants and flowers. Encourage partners to invite each other over to look at plants in their homes and yards.

● Create an after-school program (even if it meets only one afternoon each week) for adults to tutor young people, set up a homework study space, and teach young people new skills (such as using a computer, playing an instrument, studying the different types of butterflies).

Ideas for Community Outreach to Instill a Commitment to Learning

● Donate books to community and school libraries. Survey the quality of books at libraries. For example, some libraries may be short on Christian books; some may need classic books replaced.

● If your church has or supports a parochial school, explore how to integrate asset building into the school's mission and strategy. Search Institute has a major initiative to encourage schools to engage in asset building.[14]

● Advocate for high-quality, caring schools.

● Encourage your community to survey young people to learn more about them.[15]

● Set up a church library and train teenagers to staff it.

● Develop educational programs and activities that support children and youth, such as homework hot lines, tutoring, study places, and after-school programs.

NOTES

1. Susan Harter, "A New Self-Report Scale of Intrinsic Versus Extrinsic Orientation in the Classroom: Motivational and Informational Components," Developmental Psychology 17 (1981): 300-312.

2. Eugene C. Roehlkepartain, The Teaching Church: Moving Christian Education to Center Stage (Nashville, TN: Abingdon, 1993), 121-128.

3. Peter C. Scales and Nancy Leffert, Developmental Assets: A Synthesis of the Scientific Research on Adolescent Development (Minneapolis: Search Institute, 1999).

4. Diane Heacox, Up From Underachievement (Minneapolis: Free Spirit, 1991), 22.

5. Bettye M. Caldwell and Robert H. Bradley, Manual for the Home Observation for Measurement of the Environment (Little Rock: University of Arkansas Press, 1984).

6. Robert H. Bradley, Bettye M. Caldwell, and Stephen L. Rock, "Home Environment and School Performance: A Ten-Year Follow-Up Examination of Three Models of Environmental Action," Child Development 59 (1988): 852-867.

7. For more information, see Eugene C. Roehlkepartain, The Teaching Church, which is based on the Effective Christian Education study.

8. Kathy McNamara, "Bonding to School and the Development of Responsibility," Journal of Emotional and Behavioral Problems 4, no. 4 (1996): 33-35.

9. Eugene C. Roehlkepartain, The Teaching Church.

10. Richard C. Anderson et al., Becoming a Nation of Readers (Washington, DC: National Institute of Education, U.S. Department of Education, 1985).

11. Barbara D. DeBaryshe, "Joint Picture-Book Reading Correlates of Early Oral Language Skills," Journal of Child Language 20, no. 2 (1993): 455-461.

12. Mary R. Jalongo and Melissa A. Renck, "Children's Literature and the Child's Adjustment to School," Reading Teacher 40, no. 7 (1987): 616-621.

13. "Religious Leaders Pledge to Support the America Reads Challenge," U.S. Department of Education Community Update (June 1997). For information on the America Reads Challenge, call 1-800-USA-LEARN.

14. Three introductory resources are available on asset building in schools: Neal Starkman, Peter C. Scales, and Clay Roberts, Great Places to Learn: How Asset-Building Schools Help Students Succeed (Minneapolis: Search Institute, 1999); "You Have to Live It" Building Developmental Assets in School Communities (video) (Minneapolis: Search Institute, 1999); and Donald Draayer and Eugene C. Roehlkepartain, Learning and Living: How Asset Building for Youth Can Unify a School's Mission (Minneapolis: Search Institute, 1997).

15. Search Institute offers the Attitudes and Behaviors survey of young people, which measures the assets of young people in grades six to twelve in a community.

Workshops That Make Parents

WANT TO COME BACK FOR MORE

All workshops and classes are not created equal. Not only does the content you include need to be relevant to parents, but the processes you use will make a big difference in how well parents learn and whether they will be eager to participate the next time. Here are seven tips for designing and leading effective educational experiences for parents.

☐ 1. Create a supportive, caring environment for learning. Greet parents, provide time for them to get acquainted with one another, and encourage mutual support during and after the experience.

☐ 2. Actively engage parents in the learning. The amount they learn will be in direct proportion to how much they put into the experience.

☐ 3. Let parents be the experts. Show that you value their knowledge and experience by giving them opportunities to contribute to the learning experience.

☐ 4. Tie the learning activities around parents' experiences and values so they know "this is for me and about my family."

☐ 5. Focus the content on real needs, issues, and concerns, not just on content that parents ought to know. If, for example, you want to address nurturing positive values, first identify the ways this connects with parents' needs or concerns regarding values, then develop the experience to reflect those concerns.

☐ 6. Include information and skills parents can put into action immediately. Such application reinforces and helps parents internalize what they learn.

☐ 7. Pay attention to logistics. Schedule a time that is convenient for parents. Always begin and end on time. Be sure positive opportunities are available for their children during the class or workshop.

Creative Ways Volunteers and Teachers CAN LEARN

You don't have to do all the training of volunteers and teachers in your congregation by yourself. Here are some possible resources, many of which are free or inexpensive.

Workshops in the community—Take a team of volunteers from your congregation to workshops in your community sponsored by interfaith groups, secular children and youth organizations, colleges, universities, and seminaries. Or see if your team can join in a staff development training that another organization is offering to its own staff and volunteers.

People within the congregation—Don't overlook people in the congregation who have talents and gifts that could be shared. These may include teachers, counselors, professional trainers, parent educators, and many others.

Children and youth workers in other congregations—By networking with people from other congregations in your community, you will learn about programs that have been successful for them as well as particular skills they have. Consider bartering time: They can train volunteers in your congregation on a particular topic area, and you can train in their congregation on another topic.

Denominational resource people—Your denomination or association may have particular resource people assigned to congregations. Check if they have areas of expertise that match your volunteers' needs and interests.

Children and youth workers in other organizations—People who work in organizations such as the YMCA, YWCA, and Boys and Girls Clubs of America often have expertise and experience in many areas related to asset building and may be willing to help train your volunteers.

Shared learning—One of the best ways to learn new information and skills is to teach them to others. Consider forming a shared learning team (like a seminar) in which each person investigates new topics, finds and synthesizes good sources of information, and then trains the others in what he or she has learned.

Print and video resources—Design a training event based on high-quality magazine articles, books, videos, and other resources you have in your library. (Then offer to do the same training event in another congregation!)

Meeting Topics

FOR CHILDREN AND YOUTH GROUPS

This chart illustrates how each category of developmental assets can be integrated into the programming topics in congregational children's ministry or youth group.

ASSET CATEGORY	MEETING TOPICS FOR CHILDREN	MEETING TOPICS FOR YOUTH
Support	• Who is my neighbor? • Choosing a caring friend • Talking to parents • Caring school and caring church • Favorite caring adults	• Getting along with parents • Friendship issues • Getting along with adults • Showing people you care • Where to go when you need help

Empowerment	• Look what I can do!
	• How children can help and
	   make a difference
	• Keeping safe
		• Learning about your gifts and talents
		• How youth can make a difference
		   in their families, communities,
		   and world

Boundaries and Expectations	• Listening to parents • Finding and being a good friend • What's expected of me?	• Issues such as sexuality, alcohol and other drugs, violence • Positive peer pressure

Constructive Use of Time	• Fun, creative activities
	   to do at church
	• Worthwhile clubs at church
	• Why we worship God
	• What's too busy and what's not?
		• How to find balance in your life
		• The importance of staying
		   involved in the congregation
		• Art, music, and literature in
		   your faith tradition

Commitment to Learning	• Learning about God • Worthwhile reading • Feeling good about school • Why learning is fun	• Your faith and school • Choosing a college or vocational school • Finding your vocation or career
Positive Values	• Caring for the homeless • Why the truth is always best • Taking responsibility • Healthy body: God's good gift	• What your faith tradition says about service and justice • What values are important to you • What is integrity? (or honesty, etc.)
Social Competencies	• Choices, choices • Dealing with feelings (or a specific feeling) • Cooperating with others	• How to make good decisions • Friendship-making skills • Other cultures and religions • Conflict resolution
Positive Identity	• When I grow up • Feeling good about being me • What makes me special?	• What does the future hold for you? • Finding your sense of purpose in life

Instilling Positive Values

Positive values are important internal compasses to guide young people's priorities and choices. Though there are many positive values that various traditions seek to nurture in children and youth, the asset framework focuses on six widely shared values. Many others could be added. These six values can be grouped into two categories:

- The first two assets are *prosocial values* that involve caring for others and the world. For the well-being of any society, children and teenagers need to learn how and when to suspend personal gain in order to enhance the welfare of others.

- The four remaining assets focus on *personal character*, though they clearly have societal implications. These values provide a foundation for wise decision making.

All six of the positive-values assets resonate with Christianity, which emphasizes service, compassion, and justice in the world, and an ethical lifestyle guided by personal values. By nurturing positive values, congregations not only help to shape young people's life choices, but also reinforce some of the values that are central to the faith. These values also lay a foundation for discussions of life choices young people face regarding sexuality, alcohol and other drugs, and other current issues and concerns.

Many things shape young people's values. In fact, researchers Peter C. Scales and Nancy Leffert write, "Adolescents' values are molded by everything they are and do." Yet, the researchers conclude, two strategies are critical for developing positive values:

- Expectations—"Adults need to ask young people explicitly to behave in ways that reflect the underlying values adults wish youth would develop."

- Consistency—"Adults in different parts of young people's lives—school, family, congregation, neighborhood—need to be consistent in their collective expression of an explicit set of value expectations for youth."

The authors conclude: "When adults in young people's lives hold similar positive values, make these values explicit, and intentionally seek to promote them, they provide a solid guiding influence that helps youth navigate through their social worlds and internalize positive values."[1]

ASSET #26:

Caring

Caring for others is a foundational value for relationships and society. Indeed, the well-being of society rests on all people caring for each other and knowing how and when to suspend their own personal gain to help others.

Caring for others builds on the experience of being cared for yourself. Research has shown that parental warmth and affection enhances the caring in children and teenagers.[2] Children and teenagers will imitate adults who model helpfulness, generosity, and honesty. While younger children won't completely understand the pain of others, they can show their care. The ability to be truly empathetic and caring develops during the teenage years.

Congregations can do a lot to build the value of caring in children and youth. Service projects and mission projects are programmatic ways to do this. Creating a congregational atmosphere of caring in which people are expected to notice when others are missing and to reach out to those who may be in pain are other important ways to build this asset. Children can make get-well cards for sick members of the congregation. Teenagers can visit bedridden members.

Search Institute researchers have found that 43 percent of all young people report having asset #26: caring. While 54 percent of girls say they have this asset, only 32 percent of guys say they do. Tenth and eleventh grades are particular low points for guys—only 27 percent of guys in these grades report having this asset.

Equality and Social Justice

Congregations that place a high value on equality, reducing poverty and hunger, and other social justice concerns are more likely to expose children and teenagers to these values. Congregations can create ways for their youngest children to value equality and social justice by sponsoring projects in which children can help reduce hunger.

Families have lots of influence in instilling this value in their children and teenagers. In families that value equality, each family member is likely to be treated fairly. Families who do not value equality often place a greater emphasis on adults than on children. Although parents are the adults in the household, families that value equality will treat each family member with respect and fairness.

Trevor Ferrell was eleven years old when he saw a news story about people who were homeless. He begged his parents to drive him to downtown Philadelphia to hand out pillows and blankets to the homeless. By the time he was sixteen, Trevor and his parents had opened a thirty-three-room shelter called Trevor's Place, where homeless people could stay. Because Trevor's parents valued equality and social justice, they allowed Trevor to follow his passion and develop the value for his own.[3]

The Positive-Values Assets

Asset #26: Caring 43%

Asset #27: Equality and social justice 45%

Asset #28: Integrity 64%

Asset #29: Honesty 63%

Asset #30: Responsibility 60%

Asset #31: Restraint 42%

AN ASSET-BUILDING CONGREGATION

Acting in Caring Ways

Children, youth, and adults build asset #26 (caring) through an intergenerational church event at St. Bartholomew's Episcopal Church in Baltimore. The church linked up with other inner city congregations to put together kits for children in foster care. When they finished that project, they collected items for the local food pantry and then hosted a book sale. They gave all the proceeds from the book sale to help neighborhood children in their inner-city neighborhoods.

Search Institute researchers found that 45 percent of all young people report having asset #27: equality and social justice. While 57 percent of all girls say they have this asset, only 33 percent of boys report having this asset. Sixth-graders are most likely to have this asset. A decline begins in seventh grade until only 39 percent of young people say they have this asset in eleventh grade.

ASSET #28:

Integrity

People with integrity are those who have a sense of moral reflective-ness, who keep their commitments, and who are unashamed of doing the right things, says Stephen L. Carter, a Yale University professor and author of the book *Integrity*.[4] Adults and parents who have integrity act on their convictions and stand up for their beliefs. Older children and teenagers are often quick to point out when adults give mixed messages and act in ways that lack integrity.

Yet, all children—even the youngest of children—are learning about how to act with integrity by the way the adults act around them. Children and teenagers develop integrity slowly through watching the people around them and by practicing behaving in these ways.

We uphold Christian leaders when they act with integrity, and we're well aware when they don't act this way. Former President Jimmy Carter, an active Christian,

has been revered lately as a model of integrity by working toward world peace and volunteering many hours with Habitat for Humanity; in addition, he teaches Sunday school. Yet, while being a person of integrity is something we want everyone in the congregation to strive toward, we are human and sometimes slip up. These are important issues to discuss when teaching children and teenagers about integrity.

Search Institute researchers found that 64 percent of all young people say they have asset #28: integrity. While 71 percent of all girls report having this asset, only 56 percent of all guys say they have it. The older young people get, the more likely they are to report having this asset. By twelfth grade, 67 percent of guys say they have integrity, and 82 percent of girls say they do.

ASSET #29:

Honesty

Children learn about the value of honesty by being around adults who value and act in honest ways. At first, all children will make decisions impulsively to meet their immediate needs. They need guidance in how to be less impulsive and to be honest. For example, a child sneaking cookies may lie or blame another child when he or she gets caught. As teachers, adults, and parents model and teach honesty, they need to be patient with children's impulsive actions and their tales to protect themselves.

Teachers and parents can encourage children to think about their actions in order to understand what they are capable of doing rather than acting impulsively and spontaneously.

Older children and teenagers often become much more aware of the complexity of honesty, especially when they observe how common it is for people to tell white lies. White lies are often told to spare someone's feelings. Young people need to be taught how to be truthful, yet also tactful. It's much easier to respond to a person who is overweight who asks about her or his weight by saying, "No, you're not that heavy." It's harder to say something like, "I like you and don't want to hurt your feelings, but I think if you lost a few pounds you might feel better."

Ninety-two percent of high school students say they have lied to a parent, and 78 percent admit they have lied to a parent two times or more, researchers say.[5] This same study reported that religious teenagers lie less often, but still too often. While 73 percent of high school students who say religion isn't important admit to cheating on exams, so do 69 percent of young people who say religion is important.[6]

Search Institute researchers found that 63 percent of all young people say they have asset #29: honesty. While 69 percent of girls report having this asset, 56 percent of guys do. Eighth grade is the low point for young people of all ages in having this asset.

ASSET-BUILDING CONGREGATIONS PARTNER TOGETHER

Promoting Positive Values

It may not be unusual for congregations in a community to work together on something called The Year of Values. It could easily be an effort sponsored by a national interfaith or ecumenical organization. But it is unusual for schools, grocery stores, and other institutions in a community to work with local congregations in launching such a focus.

That's what happened in Northfield, Minnesota, a college town in the southern part of the state. The school district and the community's ministerial association worked together to identify and promote seven important values: equality, self-control, promise keeping, responsibility, respect, honesty, and social justice. Then others began joining in. Some of the developments in Northfield as a result of this emphasis include:

- elementary children designing posters about four key values: giving, honesty, respect, and responsibility;

- a grocery store printing information about The Year of Values on fifty thousands grocery bags;

- the parent-teacher organization offering workshops to help parents learn how to talk with their children about values;

- congregations throughout the community featuring sermons on each of the key values, culminating a month later in an ecumenical Thanksgiving service; and

- a national speaker coming to town to talk about the media and values.

Concerns about religion in schools are always present in these kinds of initiatives. But, says Northfield school superintendent Charles Kyte: "This is not teaching religion in schools. This is just helping kids and families know that values are important."

Most concerns eased as the initiative became concrete and people saw the values being promoted. In fact, it was so successful the first year that the community launched The Year of Values 2: Civility and Respect.

ASSET #30:

Responsibility

Children learn the value of responsibility early in their lives by the way their behavior affects other people. While toddlers may not understand why throwing blocks is unacceptable, they do see how a playmate reacts when hit with a block. A third-grader will see the frown on a Sunday school teacher's face when she doesn't finish her assignment. A tenth-grader will understand the importance of his attendance when he doesn't show up, and it causes his high school baseball team to forfeit a game.

Monitoring young people and being consistent with consequences is an important component of teaching young people responsibility. Researchers have found that permissive parenting or a lack of parental monitoring (asset #11: family boundaries) is strongly associated with teenage delinquency.[7] Yet monitoring alone doesn't teach children and teenagers responsibility. Adults also need to give young people meaningful, age-appropriate activities to learn personal responsibility.

Congregations can teach young people responsibility by letting children grow into taking full responsibility. At first, young children may only be parents' helpers. For example, young children can assist their parents in passing out bulletins before a worship service. As children grow older, they can handle more responsibility. Adults can gradually shift responsibility to the child. For example, elementary children can distribute bulletins before a worship service (guided by an adult), and responsible senior high youth can coordinate the schedules of young people assisting in worship by collecting the offering, greeting, and leading in readings.

Search Institute researchers found that 60 percent of all young people report having asset #30: responsibility. While 65 percent of girls say they have this asset, only 55 percent of guys say they do. Eighth grade appears to be the low point for young people in taking responsibility. While 60 percent of eighth-grade girls report having this asset, only 50 percent of eighth-grade guys do.

ASSET #31:

Restraint

A key value for young people is restraint—the internal belief that keeps them from taking unhealthy risks, such as engaging in early sexual activity or using alcohol or other drugs. While this asset focuses on believing it's "against my values" to drink alcohol or have sex while a teenager, the attitude of restraint because of what you believe shapes many other choices as well. "Hence," writes Search Institute President Peter L. Benson, "The sexual-restraint value may represent a larger commitment by young people to avoid health-compromising risks."[8]

Of the six positive-values assets, restraint (asset #31) is the one that young people are least likely to have. Overall, 42 percent of all young people report having this asset, Search Institute researchers found. While 48 percent of all girls say they have this asset, only 37 percent of guys do. This asset also experiences a large drop between sixth and twelfth grade. While 71 percent of sixth-graders say they have this asset, only 21 percent of twelfth-graders say they do.

This asset is much more common among religiously active youth. In fact, young people who participate in religious community are twice as likely as uninvolved youth to report having this asset (52 percent versus 26 percent).

However, even among the religious youth, almost half do not report having this asset. Part of the problem may be that few churches directly address these tough issues with youth. A Search Institute study of 3,100 mainline Protestant youth found that only 41 percent said they had spent six or more hours *in their lifetime* learning about or discussing sex, and just 43 percent had spent that much time learning about or discussing alcohol and other drugs. Furthermore, only 37 percent said their church did a good or excellent job of helping them learn "responsible values and behaviors in the area of sexuality."[9]

Ideas for All Ministries to Instill Positive Values

● Be clear and articulate about the values that are important to your congregation. Give people opportunities to talk about them.

● Through trips, speakers, service projects, and simulations make community and world issues personally relevant to children and youth.

● Encourage adults to model responsibility, compassion, and integrity for children and youth.

● Declare a year of values as a theme for your congregation. Invite children and youth to participate in meaningful ways.

● Feature sermons on each of the six positive-values assets, and develop an event afterward for all generations to celebrate your congregation's values.

● Honor and affirm all church members who help others and act in caring ways.

Ideas for Church Nurseries to Instill Positive Values

● Love and care for children in your nursery care unconditionally. This lays the groundwork for children to learn to care for others.

● Meet infants' and toddlers' needs for nutritious food, adequate rest, love, and a good mix of play and rest. Meeting these needs helps children develop a healthy sense

of self, which helps them develop healthy lifestyle choices and sexual attitudes as they grow older.

● Find volunteers who value and act on their positive values. Surround children with people with integrity.

● Value each child equally and delight in her or his uniqueness. This promotes asset #27: equality and social justice.

● Be honest with parents when infants and toddlers have had a difficult time in your care. Be loving in your observations while you ask questions and explain the different techniques you used to soothe the child.

Ideas for Children's Ministry to Instill Positive Values

● Model positive values by the way you act around children. For example, answer children's questions honestly. Treat all children with respect.

● Set clear expectations for what values you want children to live by. Talk about those values. Learn Bible stories about values. Highlight times when you see people living out those values— and times when those values are being honored.

● Discover the connections between setting appropriate boundaries and expectations (assets #11-#16) and instilling positive values in children

AN ASSET-BUILDING CONGREGATION

Feeding the Hungry

Three- to six-year-olds at Peachtree Road United Methodist Church in Atlanta were surprised to learn that many people go to bed hungry. So they raised money to buy an animal—a chicken, a rabbit, a bee, a pig, a goat, or a cow from Heifer Project International—to send to a hungry family somewhere in the world.

Children submitted names for the animal they wanted to purchase. The first year the class wanted to buy a pig and chose the name "Petunia Pig." Children made piggy banks to save their coins during Lent.

The second year the children wanted to buy a goat and chose the name "Velveeta." The children raised enough money to buy two goats. The class named the second goat "Feta."

(assets #26-#31). These two asset categories go hand in hand.

● Create service projects so that children not only experience what it's like to help others but also how to talk about and evaluate their experience and the values they've learned.

● Affirm the healthy choices and decisions that children make. Encourage children to create posters that promote healthy lifestyles (and build asset #31) and discourage alcohol, smoking, and drug use. Post these around your church building.

● Encourage and expect volunteers to be honest about their feelings, their successes, and their mistakes. Create a climate of honesty and caring.

● Honor and recognize children who serve others in caring ways.

Ideas for Youth Ministry to Instill Positive Values

● Regularly talk with young people about their values and the values of their friends. Give them a chance to talk it out when they're struggling to put their values into practice.

● Make youth group meetings relevant to young people by tying the learning to their life experiences and to emphasize the values at stake.

● Have Bible studies that focus on specific positive values, such as honesty and social justice.

● Whenever you notice, learn about, or hear about someone who acts with integrity, point this out to the young people in your youth ministry. Constantly uphold positive role models who have positive values.

● Have clear expectations that all guys and girls will relate respectfully and in caring ways in all youth group activities.

● Give young people opportunities to act on their values and beliefs.

Ideas for Family Ministry to Instill Positive Values

● Send home discussion questions that allow parents and children to talk about values that are raised in the media or in current events.

● Help parents get comfortable talking with children about their own beliefs and values, including values related to alcohol and other drug use and to sexuality.

● Have a family ministry activity where family members rank the six positive values (assets #26-#31) in order of importance. Have family members compare lists, and encourage them to talk about why they think some values are more important than others.

● Teach families about the connection between your faith tradition and positive values.

● Organize family activities that help poor and disadvantaged families. For example, set up a time when families can serve a meal at a community soup kitchen.

Ideas for Christian Education to Instill Positive Values

● Create warm, caring environments in all Christian education classrooms so young people feel cared for.

● Keep parents informed and involved in your teaching of values. See parents as partners in teaching.

● Create a chart listing the six positive values in the far left corner. In the middle column, have students brainstorm about what could happen if the specific value isn't followed. (Do this for each of the six assets.) In the last column, write what students say could happen if each value was honored. Compare lists and discuss.

● Develop a peer ministry program through your congregation so that children and youth can learn the skills to care for their peers. Also teach young people to know when to ask for adults' help.

● Create a list of books, videos, and books on tape that promote or reinforce the six positive values. Make these lists available for families.

CHAPTER 8

Ideas for Intergenerational Ministry to Instill Positive Values

- Address in sermons how the positive values of your faith tradition inform and shape the daily choices young people make.

- Remind all members of your congregation that they are role models of positive values for children and youth in the congregation and beyond.

- Create small groups with adults, youth, and children to discuss alcohol, drugs, and other harmful substances. (Connect it to learning about asset #31.) Have groups give reports to the large group.

- Work within your congregation in naming and reinforcing shared values for children and youth.

- Create intergenerational groups that participate in neighborhood rehabilitation projects. Find age-appropriate tasks for which children and youth can take responsibility.

Ideas for Community Outreach to Instill Positive Values

- Join with other organizations to identify and promote shared community values.

- Highlight positive values in activities sponsored for community children and youth.

- Honor young people in the community who model positive values. Consider sponsoring a scholarship or award for young people who exhibit a strong commitment to serving others.

- Make brochures available at your community center and town hall on service and relief organizations within your community. Have congregational members volunteer to serve in these organizations from time to time.

- Encourage community health professionals to give workshops to parents and children about alcohol, sex, and drugs.

NOTES

1. Peter C. Scales and Nancy Leffert, *Developmental Assets: A Synthesis of the Scientific Research on Adolescent Development* (Minneapolis: Search Institute, 1999), 171.

2. Marian Radke-Yarrow and Carolyn Zahn-Waxler, "The Role of Familial Factors in the Development of Prosocial Behavior: Research Findings and Questions," in Dan Olweus, Jack Block, and Marian Radke-Yarrow, eds., *Development of Antisocial and Prosocial Behavior* (Orlando, FL: Academic, 1986).

3. Frank and Janet Ferrell, *Trevor's Place: The Story of the Boy Who Brings Hope to the Homeless* (San Francisco: Harper and Row, 1990).

4. Stephen L. Carter, *Integrity* (New York: Basic, 1996), 7.

5. A survey of ten thousand tenth-, eleventh- and twelfth-graders by the Josephson Institute of Ethics in Patricia Edmonds, "America's Escalating Honesty Crisis," USA Weekend (October 16-18, 1998): 14.

6. Edmonds, "America's Escalating Honesty Crisis."

7. Laurence Steinberg, "Familial Factors in Delinquency: A Developmental Perspective," Journal of Adolescent Research 2, no. 3 (1987): 255-268.

8. Peter L. Benson, *All Kids Are Our Kids* (San Francisco: Jossey-Bass, 1997), 50.

9. Eugene C. Roehlkepartain and Peter L. Benson, *Youth in Protestant Churches: A Special Search Institute Report* (Minneapolis: Search Institute, 1993): 109, 111.

Integrating Responsibility
FOR YOUNG PEOPLE THROUGH LEADERSHIP

Use this matrix model to integrate age-specific concerns within each programmatic area in the congregation. You can build a leadership committee structure using this model with ten people on each committee: six adults, two youth, and two children. Young people are more apt to speak up and contribute when they have another peer with them.

Committee Member	Worship	Education	Missions	Property	Fellowship
Child's name					
Child's name					
Youth's name					
Youth's name					
Adult's name					
Adult's name					
Adult's name					
Adult's name					
Adult's name					
Adult's name					

Values and Choices

Everyone needs positive values. There is a growing consensus that personal standards are central to individual and congregational decision making. Yet, which values are important? Some values are important to certain groups of people while others are affirmed by nearly everyone. The six positive values that Search Institute names are universal values. Your congregation may have some additional values that it claims.

The six key positive values named by Search Institute include:

1. **Caring**—Young person places a high value on helping other people.

2. **Equality and social justice**—Young person places a high value on promoting equality and reducing hunger and poverty.

3. **Integrity**—Young person acts on convictions and stands up for her or his beliefs.

4. **Honesty**—Young person tells the truth even when it is not easy.

5. **Responsibility**—Young person accepts and takes personal responsibility.

6. **Restraint**—Young person believes it's important not to be sexually active or to use alcohol or other drugs.

When young people are making decisions based on their values, they can ask themselves these key questions:

● Is this a risky situation?

● Am I being pressured?

● How would my parents feel about this?

● Is this consistent with my values?

● What effect will this have on my future?

● What other choices do I have?

Building Essential Skills

Search Institute has identified a number of essential skills called social competencies that young people need to put their commitments, values, and beliefs into practice. These competencies are essential tools for helping young people confront new situations, interact well with others, and put their values and decisions into practice. Two of the social-competency assets (planning and decision making, and resistance skills) emphasize personal choices. The other three (interpersonal competence, cultural competence, and peaceful conflict resolution) focus more on healthy interpersonal relationships.

A lack of skills in both areas among many teenagers raises troubling questions about how well young people are equipped for life. Research by Father Flanagan's Boys' Home in Boys Town, Nebraska, has found a lack of social skills to be strongly linked to aggression and antisocial behavior, juvenile delinquency, child abuse and neglect, mental health disorders, loneliness and despondency, and learning disabilities and school failure.[1] Tom Dowd of Boys Town concludes:

"Youth need to become increasingly skilled as they face the developmental tasks of adolescence, such as identity and value formation, independence from family, and appropriate group affiliation. Without a strong social and psychological base from which to develop, many adolescents fail to negotiate these tasks successfully."[2]

Congregations have many opportunities to nurture social competencies in children and youth, ranging from providing leadership and service opportunities that focus on these skills to including skills development as a component of their curriculum.

For example, in talking about expectations regarding the use of alcohol or other drugs, discussions can include specific skills young people need to resist pressure from peers and the media. Similarly, discussions of racial reconciliation can include an emphasis on skills for communication and understanding across differences among people.

ASSET #32:

Planning and Decision Making

Researchers now speculate that young people's ability to solve problems relies heavily on their planning and decision-making skills.[3] When children are young, these skills need to be nurtured, then reinforced, strengthened, and deepened throughout childhood and adolescence.

Involving children in decisions that affect them not only builds their skills but also increases their sense of empowerment and competence. As children become teenagers, adults should give them even more challenging decisions to make while supporting young people in the choices they make. It's a tricky balance. Sometimes adults can give young people too little practice in making decisions or err in the opposite direction by asking them to make decisions that they're not ready for.

Churches can give young people lots of practice in making decisions. In children's ministry or Christian education classes, children can be asked to vote between two or three appealing service projects for the group to do. In youth groups teenagers can take on more leadership positions and make decisions that would make youth group meetings more appealing to young people.

Young people in churches are interested in learning to make good decisions. Search Institute's surveys of 3,100 Protestant youth found that 68 percent are interested in learning from their church about how to make decisions about what is right and wrong. Furthermore, 59 percent of these youth say their church does a good or excellent job of helping them learn to make these decisions. Yet only half of these youth (49 percent) said their church does a good or excellent job of learning how to apply their faith to everyday decisions.[4]

Of the five social competency assets, planning and decision making (asset #32) is the least common among youth surveyed. Only 29 percent of the young people surveyed report having this asset.

ASSET #33:

Interpersonal Competence

Developing the skills to interact well with people takes years of practice. While one-to-one interactions are important, so are group social situations. Children learn social skills by being with adults who love, care for, and play with them. Teenagers also learn how to interact with others by watching adults and by practicing skills with their peers.

There are two basic dimensions to the interpersonal competence asset. The first is empathy, caring about other people's feelings. The second is friendship skills. Basic friendship and relationship skills (such as courtesy, listening, seeking help, showing affirmation and care, and negotiation) are critical skills for forming positive, healthy relationships. Even for adults, these skills often need to be refined from time to time. Developing this wide range of skills is complex. Leaders and parents must be patient as young people learn these skills.

Search Institute researchers found that 43 percent of all young people report having asset #33: interpersonal competence. Girls are much more likely than guys to say they have this asset. While 43 percent of girls report having this asset, only 26 percent of guys say they do. During eighth grade, girls experience a low point regarding this asset; guys' low point is ninth grade.

The Social-Competencies Assets

29%
Asset #32: Planning and decision making

43%
Asset #33: Interpersonal competence

35%
Asset #34: Cultural competence

37%
Asset #35: Resistance skills

44%
Asset #36: Peaceful conflict resolution

ASSET #34:

Cultural Competence

Young people who have knowledge of people of different cultures and ethnic backgrounds and feel comfortable with them must first develop an ethnic awareness and cultural identity of their own. In addition, not identifying with their own cultural heritage can result in ostracism for young people, particularly for youth from minority cultures.[5]

Researchers say that children between the ages of six and eight begin to develop an awareness of the differences and similarities among children of other races. Yet it's not uncommon for preschoolers to notice differences in color of people's skin and in how people with disabilities get around in comparison to people who don't have disabilities. Responding calmly and with information about differences can help young people grow up to be comfortable and accepting of a wide variety of people.

Congregations can foster cultural competence by celebrating the diversity within your community and your world. Some congregations do this by exposing young people to missionaries who work in other countries. Other congregations intentionally reach out to the community to create a rich diversity within its membership. What's important is for congregations to expose children and teenagers to people and customs of various cultures and form strong, caring relationships with a diverse group of people.

Search Institute researchers found that 35 percent of all young people say they have asset #34: cultural competence. Girls are much more likely than guys to report having this asset. While 43 percent of girls say they have this asset, only 26 percent of boys say they do. As young people grow up, their comfort level with diversity goes down. Sixth-graders are more likely than twelfth-graders to have the asset of cultural competence.

ASSET #35:

Resistance Skills

Young people who have resistance skills and can say no or resist participating in an unacceptable or dangerous behavior are more likely to grow up healthy than are children and teenagers who don't have these skills. Resistance skills are an important ingredient in alcohol and other drug prevention programs.[6] Researchers have identified at least four dimensions to developing resistance skills:

- **Social influence**—Young people are more likely to resist negative behavior when they hear consistent messages from others (peers, parents, and the media, for example) that expect positive behavior.

- **Information**—Young people also have stronger resistance skills when they have good information about the sources of pressure to engage in negative behaviors.

- **Positive peer influence (asset #15)**—Young people are more likely to resist negative behaviors when they believe their peers, parents, and others disapprove or do not engage in the negative behaviors.

- **Self efficacy, or personal power (see asset #37)**—Young people are more likely to resist negative behaviors when they believe they actually can resist the pressure to engage in negative behaviors.[7]

Conversations about resistance skills can be difficult in the church because they require open, honest conversations about difficult topics. Young people need solid information. They need to ask questions. Many areas in which we want young people to develop resistance skills are areas that we don't talk about much in the church. Fewer than half of the Protestant youth surveyed by Search Institute said they had spent at least six hours in their lifetime talking about alcohol or other drugs (43 percent) and sexuality (41 percent).[8]

Search Institute researchers found that 37 percent of all young people have asset #35: resistance skills. While 42 percent of girls say they have this asset, only 32 percent of guys say they do.

ASSET #36:

Peaceful Conflict Resolution

Conflict-resolution skills are difficult to master, and many adults don't have these skills. Part of the challenge is that patterns of conflict resolution begin in early childhood. In fact, childhood aggression is a good predictor of delinquent behavior later in life.

One key to a child's developing conflict resolution skills depends on how the parent and other adults respond to a child's early expression of violence and aggression. Withdrawing from a biting baby and redirecting the aggressive behavior of a toddler are good strategies to set the stage for peaceful conflict resolution skills.

Although many young people have conflict with parents and other adults around them, it's the "conflicts that occur frequently and are not resolved that have the most negative effects," say Search Institute researchers. "Learning to deal with conflicts in peaceful and constructive ways is central to young people's developing the skills to manage mature relationships later in life."[9]

Unfortunately, many children and teenagers are often told to resolve conflicts nonviolently, but are not given the skills on how to do this. When young people aren't trained how to resolve conflicts peacefully, researchers found that they tend to deal with conflict in destructive ways. When young

AN ASSET-BUILDING CONGREGATION

Connecting to the "Real World"

The "real world" for teenagers in the Brother to Brother Program operated from Liberty Hill Baptist Church in Little Rock, Arkansas, is a world of high crime, gangs, violence, and racial isolation and stereotyping. But the program—which focuses its efforts on young African American males—doesn't seek to shield participants from this real world, says program director Jimmy Cunningham. Rather, it seeks to give them the skills, support, and sense of identity they need to deal with the world around them.

The program (which receives federal, state, and other support) weaves together social rituals, cultural information, and educational enrichment within the context of values. For four days each week, fifty boys, ages six to eighteen, come together for a meal, group activities, ceremonies, tutoring, computer classes, and other programs. They watch both educational and entertainment videos, but always take time to talk about what they see. "In the context of talking about who they are, we talk about what that means in the real world," Cunningham says.

"As black males," Cunningham says, "[these young men] feel stigmatized in the school and community." He continues: "In a world that is increasingly multicultural, it becomes even more important to be comfortable and grounded in self so you can relate to other people. What we offer is a holistic kind of approach to dealing with the multitude of issues they have to deal with."

ASSET-BUILDING CONGREGATIONS

Deciding, Planning, and Making Ideas Come True

Fourteen-year-old Tim Coonen had an idea. After he started skateboarding, he didn't have a place to go. So he proposed that his confirmation class at Mountain View Lutheran Church in Phoenix create a skateboarding park.

The church agreed to provide space and a start-up loan to purchase wood for the ramps. They got the YMCA to provide staff supervision during hours of operation, and they received donations from the Rotary Club, CHADD, Lutheran Brotherhood, and CIGNA HealthCare. The young people had the park up and running within four weeks. It's now open from 1 to 5 p.m. each Friday and 10 a.m. to 5 p.m. on Saturdays.

"They came up with all the rules and ideas," says Sheila Coonen, the director of parish ministries at the church. "Now they're beginning to think of other things the community can use that the church can help create. It's helping them to realize that kids can do a lot to change their community."

people are trained with practical skills, however, they are better at negotiating and using conflict resolution strategies.[10]

Congregations can go a long way in building this asset in children and youth. But building the asset is more than telling young people to "say no" to violence (though that's part of the equation). Rather, there are several elements that build this asset:

- Early intervention and clear boundaries about aggression for young children.

- Teaching parents to model good problem-solving and conflict-resolution skills.

- Helping young people develop strong social support and interpersonal competencies (asset #33), since youth with a stronger social base are less likely to engage in aggressive behavior.

- Teaching young people skills for negotiating differences and coping with stress (since stress often triggers aggression).

Search Institute researchers found that 44 percent of all young people report having asset #36: peaceful conflict resolution. While 56 percent of girls say they have this asset, only 31 percent of guys say they do. This difference between the genders reflects the troubling levels of aggressiveness and violence among young men in this society.

Ideas for All Ministries to Build Social Competencies

- Celebrate the diversity within your congregation and the world. Have a worship service that honors diversity. Have an international potluck dinner.

- Examine the values, practices, and norms in your congregation to determine if they are truly welcoming and inclusive of people from many cultural or ethnic backgrounds.

- Have young people plan certain aspects of congregational events. For example, young people can plan some music to play, select favorite foods, and lead activities for young participants.

- Teach members how to start conversations with people who are different from them.

- Include young people in some of the planning and decision making of your congregational committees.

- Establish clear expectations regarding avoidance of negative behaviors such as drug use, violence, and premature sexual activity.

- Have workshops, service projects, and activities that focus on teaching the skills that are part of the social-competencies assets.

Ideas for Church Nurseries to Build Social Competencies

- Give infants and toddlers choices, such as choosing to eat a mashed banana or applesauce.

- Respond to conflict as soon as it occurs. Be clear about what's acceptable and not acceptable, such as saying, "No biting. No kicking. When you're mad, use your words."

- Get permission from parents to publish a directory of the children in your church nursery, which has the child's name, child's birth date (and year), address, phone number, and parents' names. This can encourage interpersonal relationships to form between families.

- Play music from other cultures, and read stories about children of many races, ethnicities, and cultures. Talk about what's the same and what's different between those children in the books and the children in your church nursery.

- Be understanding when toddlers begin to say "no, no, no" and assert themselves. This means toddlers are beginning to develop a sense of self, which will help them develop resistance skills later.

- Provide extra support and attention for families under stress, since stress can trigger violence or aggression in the family.

Ideas for Children's Ministry to Build Social Competencies

- Help children see connections between their faith and their decision making. Point out how faith informs people's decisions.

- Be interested in what children have to say. Listen to them. Encourage them to listen to others.

- Teach children the importance of resisting negative peer pressure and dangerous situations (asset #35). Give them activities to help them practice building their assertiveness skills.

- Give children time to get to know each other during church activities. They may never see each other outside of church, since they may attend different schools.

- Have a cultural costume party. Have children dress up in clothing from many cultures. Serve food from around the world.

- If you notice children who have trouble with aggression, determine whether they are feeling isolated or alone. Befriend them and help them develop other strong friendships in the church.

- Affirm how children care for each other when other children visit and when they get along with their siblings.

Ideas for Youth Ministry to Build Social Competencies

- When focusing on a topic, teach the specific skills that address the topic effectively. For example, when teaching about being friends with people who are different, talk about skills for introducing yourself to someone new and beginning to get to know each other.

- Have youth group meetings where you talk about the challenges and the rewards of maintaining relationships with people of different backgrounds, religious beliefs, and cultures.

- Involve young people in making financial decisions in youth ministry. Not only will it teach them financial skills, but it will help to build the planning and decision making asset.

- Include teenagers in planning youth group meetings and activities.

- Teach youth relationship skills, using approaches such as peer ministry training.

- Give young people opportunities to get to know people from other backgrounds and cultures. Consider linking up with a congregation of a different culture.

- Deal openly and honestly with the kinds of pressures young people face to engage in negative or risky behaviors. Find ways that young people can provide social support for each other in making positive choices.

ASSET-BUILDING CONGREGATIONS

Using Skills to Change the System

Since 1996 the faith-based Boston Youth Organizing Project (BYOP) has been developing leadership skills among seventh- to twelfth-grade youth in nineteen congregations throughout Boston. In 1997 the BYOP worked with other community organizations to convince the state of Massachusetts to open an abandoned ice-skating rink as an in-line skating rink. During the summer of 1998, the group persuaded the head of the Massachusetts Bay Transit Authority to lengthen the hours for use of school bus and train passes from 6 to 8 p.m. so students could participate in after-school activities. The passes that could be used at a later time gave young people, especially high school seniors, the opportunity to participate in after-school activities and be successful academically.

Ideas for Family Ministry to Build Social Competencies

● When offering parenting workshops, include information and skills parents can put into action immediately.

● Give parents and children opportunities to practice working through problems, conflicts, and differences in healthy ways.

● Teach parents skills for coping with challenges and stress.

● Challenge family members to articulate the reasons and values behind their decisions.

● Support programs that work to reduce domestic violence and abuse. Publish warning signs of domestic violence to keep families informed. Distribute information on how to resolve conflicts peacefully.

● Let children and youth plan a family ministry activity. Give them a budget and a time frame to follow. Help them make their plans a success. Encourage parents to support young people and not take over.

Ideas for Christian Education to Build Social Competencies

● Educate teachers about respecting, understanding, and working with children from different backgrounds and cultures.

● Help children and youth create plans to learn important aspects of their faith or key information from the Bible.

● Use the book *Sadako and the Thousand Paper Cranes* by Eleanor Coerr (or other books on origami) to tie into asset #36: peaceful conflict resolution. Teach children and youth how to fold paper cranes as described in the book. Then have young people each write a pledge for peace on their cranes. Connect the cranes in a long chain, and hang them in your classroom, hallway, or sanctuary.

● Create a listing of cultural events in your community. Distribute these lists to young people and their families.

Ideas for Intergenerational Ministry to Build Social Competencies

- Form a partnership with a congregation with a different cultural, ethnic, or religious heritage. Plan activities that allow people of all ages to learn from and about each other.

- Draw on your church's commitment to peace by highlighting for all members the importance of peaceful conflict resolution at home, in your congregation, in the community, and around the world.

- Host a variety of cultural groups for intergenerational events, such as a Japanese drum group, a Minnesota polka band, an Appalachian clogging group, and a Caribbean steel drum band.

- Whenever you plan an intergenerational event, always include one fun question that encourages people to talk to each other. For example, say, "Tell one person you don't know one thing about the house and neighborhood you lived in when you were four years old."

- Form an intergenerational committee to plan an intergenerational event. Make sure you have members representing different age groups of your church: children, youth, young adults, middle-aged adults, and seniors.

Ideas for Community Outreach to Build Social Competencies

- Include skill building in after-school activities that your congregation offers or sponsors for community young people.

- Get involved in community efforts to encourage nonviolence and peaceful conflict resolution. Support community efforts to build young people's social skills.

- Help young people develop dramatic and musical presentations for teaching social skills to children and youth in the community. Perform them in places such as parks, malls, and community centers.

- Offer sessions for young people in the community that address skill-building topics.

- Invite speakers to speak at a community event for children and youth about the power young people have in making positive choices.

Some Skills Volunteers Need

TO BE EFFECTIVE IN BUILDING ASSETS

Here is a preliminary list of the kinds of skills volunteers need to develop to be effective in nurturing each type of asset.

TO PROVIDE...	VOLUNTEERS NEED TO KNOW HOW TO...
Support	☐ greet a young person and start a conversation. ☐ listen to a young person.
Empowerment	☐ invite young people to share their gifts and talents. ☐ praise effectively.
Boundaries and Expectations	☐ discipline in a way that teaches. ☐ set limits.
Constructive Use of Time	☐ connect topics to young people's lives and interests. ☐ integrate physical activity into educational sessions.
Commitment to Learning	☐ develop activities for different learning styles. ☐ model a positive attitude toward and interest in school and learning.
Positive Values	☐ model and articulate their own values. ☐ teach problem-solving skills.
Social Competencies	☐ integrate skill building into curricula and activities. ☐ teach social skills to young people, such as listening, asking for help, negotiating, and expressing anger in acceptable ways.
Positive Identity	☐ give a compliment. ☐ help young people identify their own talents and abilities.

Equipping People With Skills
FOR ASSET BUILDING

In our enthusiasm to build assets, we may forget that many people do not have the skills they need to be part of the team. We need to stop and guide them in how to meet other people, how to form friendships, how to articulate and enforce boundaries, how to be affirming of young people, how to talk about their values. The good news is that these things can be taught and learned. Here are some ideas of what congregations can do.

☐ Whenever encouraging young people or adults to undertake a new activity, provide training or tips for how to do that activity. For example, if you are asking congregation members to get to know children and youth, include in your congregation's newsletter some tips about how to greet young people and some things they could talk about or do together. Similarly, if you ask teenagers to serve as leaders, guide them in learning the skills they need to be effective in those roles.

☐ When taking children and youth into new situations (such as a service project in which they will be with people who are different from them), coach them in advance on some basic skills they can use in those situations.

☐ When young people are struggling with a particular problem or issue, help them identify the skills they need to solve that problem. For example, if they are having difficulty getting along with a friend, what skills could they use that would help to turn the friendship around?

☐ Break larger skills into smaller, more manageable skills. If you are encouraging parents to create boundaries for their children, teach them how to set boundaries, how to keep everyone in the family informed about boundaries, how to set up consequences, how to enforce consequences consistently, and how to renegotiate boundaries as children grow.

Teaching Social Competencies

With each of the five social-competencies assets, write two example of how to teach each one to young people in your congregation. For example, young people could practice asset #32 by planning a service project, step by step from start to finish.

Social-Competencies Asset	Examples of How to Teach This Social-Competencies Asset in Your Congregation
Asset #32: Planning and Decision Making—Young person knows how to plan ahead and make choices.	
Asset #33: Interpersonal Competence—Young person has empathy, sensitivity, and friendship skills.	
Asset #34: Cultural Competence—Young person has knowledge of and comfort with people of different cultural/racial/ethnic backgrounds.	
Asset #35: Resistance Skills—Young person can resist negative peer pressure and dangerous situations.	
Asset #36: Peaceful Conflict Resolution—Young person seeks to resolve conflict nonviolently.	

NOTES

1. Tom Dowd, *Teaching Social Skills to Youth* (Boys Town, NE: Boys Town Press, 1995), 4-5.

2. Dowd, *Teaching Social Skills to Youth*, 5.

3. M. Windle et al., "Adolescent Perceptions of Help-Seeking Resources for Substance Abuse," Child Development 62 (1991): 179-189.

4. Eugene C. Roehlkepartain and Peter L. Benson, *Youth in Protestant Churches: A Special Search Institute Report* (Minneapolis: Search Institute, 1993), 89, 111.

5. J. Ogbu, "Immigrant and Involuntary Minorities in Comparative Perspective," in M.G. Gibson and J.U. Ogbu, eds., *Minority Status and Schooling*, (New York: Garland, 1991), 3-33.

6. Gilbert J. Botvin et al., "A Cognitive-Behavioral Approach to Substance Use Prevention: One Year Follow-Up," Addictive Behaviors 15 (1990): 47-63.

7. Based on research summarized in Peter C. Scales and Nancy Leffert, *Developmental Assets: A Synthesis of the Scientific Research on Adolescent Development* (Minneapolis: Search Institute, 1999), 171.

8. Roehlkepartain and Benson, *Youth in Protestant Churches*, 109.

9. Scales and Leffert, *Developmental Assets*, 185.

10. D.W. Johnson and R.T. Johnson, "Conflict Resolution and Peer Mediation Programs in Elementary and Secondary Schools: A Review of the Research," Review of Educational Research 66 (1996): 459-506.

Nurturing a Positive Identity

Identity formation is one of the critical tasks of childhood and adolescence, as young people ask the questions: "Who am I and who do I want to become?" The eighth and final category of assets focuses on young people's views of themselves—their own sense of power, purpose, and promise. Without these assets, young people can become powerless victims without a sense of initiative, direction, and purpose.

All young people develop a personal identity. Some, however, accept it passively, accepting whatever roles and self-image that others give them. Young people who form their identity passively often live life filled with uncertainty and self-doubt.

Active identity focuses on young people actively searching for and examining their own life choices and commitments. They develop a sense of self-confidence and mastery.

The positive-identity assets tie closely to a faith identity. The Christian faith offers hope, meaning, and purpose for believers. Faith can

help young people discover that they can make a difference (personal power), that they are valuable people (self-esteem), that they have a special calling or vocation (sense of purpose), and that they can have deep and abiding hope for the future (positive view of personal future).

Furthermore, the active search for and acceptance of a faith commitment is a critical element of faith

formation during adolescence, when young people enter what James Fowler describes as the stage of "synthetic-conventional faith." During this stage, young people put together the pieces of their self-concept, values, and stories. This process of integration involves testing limits, experimenting, doubting, and questioning—all of which are part of an active identity development process.[1]

Yet it is surprising, even disturbing, that young people who are active in churches are only slightly more likely to experience any of the positive identity assets. Here, again, are the percentages of active and inactive/nonreligious youth reporting each of these assets.

Asset	Religiously Active	Inactive/ Nonreligious
#37: Personal power	48%	39%
#38: Self-esteem	49%	42%
#39: Sense of purpose	58%	48%
#40: Positive view of personal future	74%	63%

Whereas the difference between religious and inactive youth on some other assets is as high as 25 percent, the largest difference on the positive identity assets is 11 percent. Given the central message of the gospel of hope, calling, and a sense of purpose, these assets should be an area where churches are contributing tremendously to young people's asset foundation.

Search Institute's previous research on Protestant youth asked a series of questions about how well the church addresses positive identity issues. Of the youth surveyed, 62 percent said the church did a good or excellent job helping them feel good about themselves (asset #38: self esteem), and 51 percent said the church did a good job of helping them gain a sense of purpose in life (asset #39: sense of purpose).[2] These responses suggest that there's a great deal of improvement possible in how churches help build the positive-identity assets.

ASSET #37:

Personal Power

Having a sense of personal control and power is critical for a positive identity. People who do not have a sense that they have power over the things that happen to them can feel helpless, passive, and victimized.

A number of Christians question this asset, saying that we should focus on God's power, not personal power. Yet this asset doesn't say that personal power is more important than God's power. Rather, the asset helps people live out *The Serenity Prayer*, written by Reinhold Neibuhr, which begins, "God, grant me the serenity to accept the things I cannot change, courage to change the things I can, and the wisdom to know the difference."

A person who feels helpless and victimized or trapped is a passive person who doesn't act on her or his faith. A person without a sense of personal power blames everything on others or circumstances and does not take personal responsibility for her or his actions. A person with personal power believes he or she can make a difference.

Children develop a sense of personal power (or the belief that they don't have any) from an early age. Adults who encourage infants to crawl, walk, and talk, are all giving infants the license to use their personal power. Adults who squash these developments, also hinder the child's spirit and belief that he or she can do worthwhile things.

Congregations can nurture this asset by giving children and youth opportunities where their contributions do make a difference. When young people pick up litter alongside a highway, they can see the results. They see how worthwhile their actions were. This encourages young people to keep trying and believing that their hard work is essential, which builds this asset.

Search Institute researchers found that 45 percent of all young people say they have this asset. Girls and guys are practically equal in saying they have this asset.

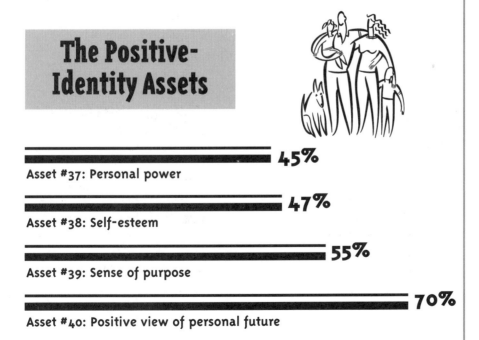

The Positive-Identity Assets

Asset #37: Personal power — 45%

Asset #38: Self-esteem — 47%

Asset #39: Sense of purpose — 55%

Asset #40: Positive view of personal future — 70%

![AN ASSET-BUILDING CONGREGATION]

Nurturing Positive Identity

"**I**mani Circle." "Kuumba Class." "Lion's Den."

While these phrases aren't common names in youth programs, they represent some of the philosophy of the Brother to Brother Program at Liberty Hills Baptist Church in Little Rock, Arkansas. The program—which serves a neighborhood facing high rates of poverty and crime—builds on a philosophy that helping African American young males recover their cultural roots and identity is critical to their healthy development.

Thus every aspect of the program is carefully designed to provide young men with the structure, support, and opportunities they need within a context of positive identity and cultural heritage. Imani Circle (named after the Swahili word for "faith") is a sharing and affirmation time. In Kuumba Class (Swahili for "creativity"), the boys make masks, molded figures, and other crafts. And the Lion's Den is a recreation room.

Cunningham says they are seeing a real difference in young men's lives. When one boy began the program, he had a 1.3 grade-point average (GPA), had been suspended for one hundred days for fighting in school, and scored low on a scale of racial identity. After one and a half years in the program, the boy has a 3.1 GPA. and his scores on the racial identity scale have improved dramatically. Cunningham concludes: "We're talking about a kid who has become much more grounded and much more rooted."

ASSET #38:

Self-Esteem

A positive sense of self is an essential component of healthy development during childhood and adolescence. When children and youth have opportunities to be involved in positive and supportive relationships, develop life skills, be part of a group, and feel they have something to contribute, their development of a sense of self-competence is enhanced.[3]

While many people talk about the importance of self-esteem, few seem to know the specifics of what builds self-esteem. Author and psychologist Dr. Louise Hart, a leading expert on self-esteem development, says high self-esteem comes from

- love, respect, and acceptance.

- being taken seriously.

- being listened to.

- having your needs met and taken seriously.

- honoring uniqueness.

- being healthy and fit.

- having meaning and purpose in life.

- having a sense of humor, laughter, and play.

- taking pride in your cultural heritage.

- having choices and a sense of personal power.

- having safety and security.

- doing good.

- feeling competent.

- making achievements.[4]

Children's and teenagers' self-esteem is affected by their feelings of self-competence in the areas they believe are important to them. For example, if playing soccer is important to a guy, but he does not feel that he is good at soccer, his self-esteem will suffer. Yet if a girl wants to be a great trombonist and she feels good about her progress in learning the instrument, her self-esteem will be strengthened.

In recent years no other subject has gained as much attention as self-esteem in education and child rearing. Indeed many people view it as the most important asset. Hundreds of books and articles have been published that say essentially what a subtitle claimed in a parenting magazine: "Self-esteem may well be the most important trait you can develop in your child."[5]

However, research by Search Institute and others finds that self-esteem, though important, is by no means the most powerful asset.[6] Rather, it is one element of a larger formula of healthy development for children and youth. Furthermore, self-esteem is not a simple concept; it involves young people's perceptions of themselves in many areas. Researchers have found that it is very difficult to change a young person's self-esteem, unless a program is unusually intensive and comprehensive.[7] So while attention to self-esteem is important, this emphasis should not overshadow a commitment to building the range of assets children and youth need.

Search Institute researchers found that 47 percent of all young people report having asset #38: self-esteem. Guys are much more likely than girls to have this asset. While 54 percent of guys say they have this asset, only 40 percent of girls say they do.

ASSET #39:

Sense of Purpose

For young people to have a sense of purpose in life, they need to look within. What gives their life meaning? Why do they get up in the morning? What dreams do they have for the future? What is God calling them to be and do in the world?

The difference between young people who have a sense of purpose and those who don't boils down to one thing: Those who do will take charge of their lives. If they're unsure of what gives them meaning or purpose, they set out to find it. If they know what gives them purpose, they are out there doing it.

Churches can play a vital role in nurturing a sense of purpose. This asset challenges churches to become partners with children and youth in discovering how God is calling them to live their lives and what God is calling them to do (vocation). Vocation isn't just about those who are called into professional ministry; it's about how each person is called to use her or his gifts in ministry through any job, family responsibilities, community involvement, personal friendships, and other ways people use their time, talents, and treasures.

Search Institute researchers found that 55 percent of all young people say they have asset #39: sense of purpose. While 60 percent of guys say they have this asset, only 50 percent of girls say they do. The low point for guys occurs during the sixth and seventh grades. For girls, it's the eighth and ninth grades.

ASSET #40:

Positive View of Personal Future

Children and teenagers develop a positive view of the future through observing others around them. When parents and adults view their own futures positively and aspire to make young people's lives full of opportunity and promise, they convey hope and optimism to children and youth.

Researcher Martin E.P. Seligman developed a pyramid of optimism to show that young people develop a positive view of the future in a progressive, three-stage process that starts in infancy.[8] The first step is mastery, which gives children a feeling of control over their environment. When children are given simple choices, they feel they have a sense of control. As children learn new skills and become good at these skills, they feel a sense of mastery. Adults can help children work through difficult situations through play to help them gain a sense of mastery, such as role-playing situations when the children get angry (being teased by others, for example) or frightened (getting a shot at the doctor's office, for example).

The second step is called positivity. Children and youth who feel loved and accepted are more likely to feel good about themselves and their futures. Seligman says adults should love young people unconditionally and praise young people contingent on their success and in doses that fit the accomplishment. When young people fail, Seligman suggests parents shouldn't look for something to praise them for but instead break the task into manageable steps and encourage young people to work toward success.

At the top of the optimism pyramid is style. This has to do with the way young people interpret the events that happen to them. Young people who view the future and the world with pessimism will blame themselves (or others) and see these failures as permanent and unchangeable. Young people who have an optimistic view of the future will see setbacks as temporary and changeable, and they will try again.

The way young people interpret the future and the world is something that can be changed. When churches are intentional about building relationships between young people and adults, adults can learn how young people think by getting to know them. Adults can question the way young people interpret events and share other ways to view setbacks and difficulties.

A healthy sense of optimism about the future can be a driving influence for young people to make positive choices. Thus, stories of children and youth who are haunted by daily violence and cycles of unending poverty become even more disturbing because they cannot be sure they even have a future. Giving these young people reason for hope represents a vital challenge to congregations.

Search Institute researchers found that 70 percent of all young people report having asset #40: positive view of personal future. Of all the assets, this is the one that's most commonly reported by young people. This level of optimism offers a tremendous resource upon which to build.

Ideas for All Ministries to Nurture a Positive Identity

- Have children and youth (or Christian education classes) take turns in leading certain parts of worship services. Give all young people the opportunity to participate, not just those who are interested or those who seem to have natural leadership skills.

- Publish a short article about a different child or teenager each week in your church bulletin. Encourage the young person to attend church services that week and recognize her or him during the service so that members can put a name with a face. During the year keep track so that each young person gets recognized.

- Accept and affirm all children and teenagers for who they are. Recognize their individual talents, abilities, and accomplishments.

- When addressing problems in the community or world, try to always offer some way for people to make a positive difference. Otherwise, you risk cultivating a sense of being overwhelmed and feeling hopeless about the future.

- Pass on to children and youth the hope that is integral to your church's beliefs.

Ideas for Church Nurseries to Nurture a Positive Identity

- Create a warm and loving environment in your nursery so that children feel safe and secure. This type of environment gives children the confidence to be who they are and to explore and grow.

- Hold children a lot. Get down on the floor and play with them. Hug them. Rub their backs. Rock them. Children who are supported in affectionate ways will develop a positive identity.

- Hang up a photo of each child in your care. Show how each infant and toddler is important. Continue to add photos as new children come to your church nursery.

- When infants get to the stage where they drop everything, play with them. Pick up what they dropped and give it to them. Most likely they'll drop it again. Make a game of this. This builds asset #37.

- Respond positively when infants and toddlers act in positive ways. When they smile, smile back at them. When they clap, clap with them.

Ideas for Children's Ministry to Nurture a Positive Identity

- Notice when children enjoy doing certain activities. Be enthusiastic about their passions.

- Create a children's hall of fame on one of your hallways. Hang up art projects and photographs of children in your church. Include something from each child.

- Develop a children's ministry vision statement about your commitment to children. Make a list of ways your ministry will work toward this commitment. Post this statement in your church.

- Occasionally send a note to a child affirming something he or she does well.

- Make sure you give optimistic, not pessimistic messages. Instead of complaining, "This is impossible!" or "All I get are problems!" say, "This is a challenge, but I'm up to it" or "This looks tricky, but I'll figure it out."

AN ASSET-BUILDING CONGREGATION

Looking to the Future

Young people at St. Michael's Catholic Church in Stillwater, Minnesota, look forward to the future because they see the leadership that grows as they grow older. Director of youth ministry Rich Junghans has college-age students come back and work with the senior high group. Teenagers from the senior high group work with young people in the junior high group. "We put them in a position to really share their knowledge," Junghans says. "And the kids seem to enjoy that. They take great pride in being able to tell their story, and it's fun to watch these kids really step up into these roles."

AN ASSET-BUILDING CONGREGATION

Helping Children Feel Good About Themselves

We want the children to gain pride in themselves, and one day be able to decide their own futures," says Lucy Wade, who works with Project SPIRIT, an after-school tutorial and life-skills program created by the Congress of National Black Churches for urban children between the ages of six and twelve.

Wade and others who greet the twenty-five children who come to Mt. Horeb Baptist Church in Washington, D.C., and do activities with them help them feel good about themselves. They focus on boosting children's academic skills and giving them the love and support they need to deal with daily experiences in ways that pave a way for a positive future.

Ideas for Youth Ministry to Nurture a Positive Identity

- As young people explore vocational and life questions, help them search for things that offer a sense of meaning, purpose, and hope.

- Help young people sort through their own sense of cultural heritage and identity.

- Have youth group meetings that encourage teenagers to talk about life goals, priorities, values, and dreams.

- Post inspiring quotes about people who have a sense of purpose (asset #39) in your church newsletter, youth group rooms, or hallways.

- Help youth discover and use their talents. Focus more on their promise and possibility than on their problems.

- Directly address issues of vocation, careers, and callings in youth programming. Help young people examine their gifts and to listen for what God is calling them to do and be.

Ideas for Family Ministry to Nurture a Positive Identity

- Provide support for families that are struggling to identify their own sources of strength and power that give them some control over their own circumstances.

- Create a family ministry directory that lists each family member's interests, hobbies, activities, and employment in addition to address and phone number. Encourage families to network with other families who have similar interests.

- Help families work through times of stress and conflict. Young people who experience stress and conflict in their homes are more likely to struggle with a sense of hope and promise for the future.

- Host an event for parents and children to talk together about their hopes and dreams for the future—as individuals and as a family.

- Provide opportunities for family members to talk about their vocational and activity choices from a faith perspective.

- Have families create a "We did it!" journal. Once a month have family members individually name things they've accomplished or things they've noticed other family members accomplish. Celebrate these successes.

Ideas for Christian Education to Nurture a Positive Identity

- Affirm the strengths and talents of each young person. Challenge young people to work on their weaknesses. Celebrate their progress and accomplishments.

- Give young people lots of hands-on experiences that allow them to create and challenge themselves. With young children, you can ask, "What would happen if you pour water into that sand hole?" when playing with sand and water. With teenagers, you can ask, "What would happen if you hum at the same time you blow into a harmonica?"

- Study the daily newspaper to find stories of individuals who have a positive view of the future and those who don't. Talk about how a person's attitude affects a person's life.

- Create question work sheets for children to use during Christian education. Ask questions that directly relate to the four positive identity assets (assets #37-#40) and encourage children to think about their beliefs, values, and attitudes.

- Study the prophets. How did they maintain a balance between addressing the serious problems and offering a hope and promise for a better future?

- Create a Christian education newspaper where each classroom contributes something meaningful. Individual classrooms can do this with each classmate contributing at least one thing to the newsletter.

Ideas for Intergenerational Ministry to Nurture a Positive Identity

- Help children, teenagers, and adults discover and share their unique gifts and talents with each other.

- Get young people to create a video or scrapbook that shows signs of hope for the future. Have them share it with the whole congregation.

- Have each person write one sentence that describes the kind of person they want to be on an 8½x11 paper. Form intergenerational small groups to talk about what each person wrote.

- Whenever you have an intergenerational event, always include a getting-to-know you discussion question, such as "Tell your small group three things about yourself that few people know about you" or "Name one thing you enjoy doing most and one thing you hate doing most."

- Have each person in your congregation trace their hands on a piece of paper and cut them out. Have them write their names on their paper hands along with activities they enjoy and words that describe them. Hang the paper hands on a wall for everyone to see.

Ideas for Community Outreach to Nurture a Positive Identity

- Sponsor or cosponsor programs or activities that help young people affirm and connect with their own cultural heritage.

- Work with community young people to paint a mural (or murals) that depict the kind of community and world they hope for.

- Invite role models from the community who have overcome the odds to talk to groups of community young people about how a sense of purpose and meaning has helped to shape their lives.

- Convene a group of guys and a group of girls to talk about what it means to be male and female today.

- Get your community to make children and youth a priority for your community's agenda. Churches often have been leaders in creating asset-building initiatives that place an emphasis on children and youth.

Talking About Movies and Videos

We live in a media-saturated society. We spend a lot of time seeing movies and videos, and they influence who we are and who we want to become (or don't want to become). Movies and videos can impact the choices that we make in terms of fashion, music, and the items we buy.

Use these ideas to direct discussion about movies and videos, especially in terms of assets, and critique them in ways that focus on asset-building themes and messages:

● Who were the role models in the movie? Who were the villains? Did those roles reflect stereotypes or generalizations about what certain races, cultures, or other groups are like? Were females and males equally represented?

● Which scene best showed people building assets for other people? Which scene showed the least amount of asset building?

● Which characters seemed to have the most assets? Which had the least? What difference did that make in the things they did and the choices they made?

● Which values did different characters in the movie have? How did those values impact their actions?

● Which characters in the movie seemed most empowered and in control of their lives? What helped them be that way?

● Which character in the movie would you most like to be? Why? Which character would you least like to be? Why?

● What are the messages in the movie about sex, alcohol and other drugs, how to resolve conflicts, money, gender, race, class, and other issues?

● Who were the characters in the movie who would support you the most if they were real people? Why? Who were the people you think would support you the least? Why?

● What would you change about the movie to give it a strong message about asset building?

Building the Positive-Identity

All young people need to feel good about themselves and their abilities. Here are ideas on how to build the four positive-identity assets for children and youth at different ages.

Birth to One Year	☐ Always love, accept, and respect babies. ☐ Play together with babies in ways that make them laugh and enjoy the time together.
One to Two Years	☐ Create a loving, supportive, and affirming atmosphere for children. ☐ Dwell on what children do right instead of what they do wrong. When they make mistakes or act out, focus on the behavior, not the child. For example, instead of saying, "No! You are so naughty," try saying, "No, it's not OK for you to do that."
Three to Five Years	☐ Break new tasks and skills into small, manageable steps that children can master without becoming too frustrated. ☐ Talk with children about the good things that happen in their lives. ☐ Find ways to teach children about their cultural heritage, through stories or special foods, for example.
Six to Eleven Years	☐ When children are facing problems or difficult times, help them think of all the possible ways they could deal with the situation. Then help them pick what they want to do. ☐ Encourage children to find inspirational, positive role models. ☐ Talk with children about what gives your life meaning and a sense of purpose.
Twelve to Fifteen Years	☐ Expect young people to experience ups and downs of self-esteem during these years and for it to increase as they get older. ☐ Avoid comparing young people with each other.
Sixteen to Eighteen Years	☐ Let teenagers know that you are proud of and excited by their talents, capabilities, and discoveries. ☐ Support teenagers as they struggle with issues and questions of identity. ☐ Let teenagers know that you are willing to listen if they want to talk about their sense of purpose in life, including their ideas about how they would like to contribute to the world.

The Nature of a Mature Faith

What are the characteristics of a person with a mature Christian faith? Based on interviews with theological scholars and denominational executives, open-ended surveys of several hundred adults from Protestant denominations across the country, and the reviews of literature in psychology and religion, Search Institute identified that a person of mature faith integrates eight core dimensions of faith:

☐ **1.** Trusts in God's saving grace and believes firmly in the humanity and divinity of Jesus.

☐ **2.** Experiences a sense of personal well-being, security, and peace.

☐ **3.** Integrates faith and life, seeing work, family, social relationships, and political choices as part of one's religious life.

☐ **4.** Seeks spiritual growth through study, reflection, prayer, and discussion with others.

☐ **5.** Seeks to be part of a community of believers in which people give witness to their faith and support and nourish one another.

☐ **6.** Holds life-affirming values, including commitment to racial and gender equality, affirmation of cultural and religious diversity, and a personal sense of responsibility for the welfare of others.

☐ **7.** Advocates for social and global change to bring about greater social justice.

☐ **8.** Serves humanity, consistently and passionately, through acts of love and justice.

For more information about faith maturity, see Eugene C. Roehlkepartain, *The Teaching Church: Moving Christian Education to Center Stage* (Nashville, TN: Abingdon, 1993).

NOTES

1. See James W. Fowler, *Becoming Adult, Becoming Christian: Adult Development and the Christian Faith* (San Francisco: Harper and Row, 1984), 67-71.

2. Eugene C. Roehlkepartain and Peter L. Benson, *Youth in Protestant Churches: A Special Search Institute Report* (Minneapolis: Search Institute, 1993), 112.

3. Richard M. Lerner, *America's Youth in Crisis: Challenge and Options for Programs and Policies* (Thousand Oaks, CA: Sage, 1995).

4. Louise Hart, *The Winning Family* (Berkeley, CA: Celestial Arts, 1993), 10.

5. Marianne Neifert, "A Strong Sense of Self," Parenting (October 1991): 98-109.

6. See Susan Harter, "Self and Identity Development," in Shirley S. Feldman and Glen R. Elliott, eds., *At the Threshold: The Developing Adolescent* (Cambridge: Harvard University Press, 1990), 353-387. Also see Alfie Kohn, "The Truth About Self-Esteem," Phi Delta Kappan (December 1994): 272-283.

7. Nancy Leffert et al., *Making the Case: Measuring the Impact of Youth Development Programs* (Minneapolis: Search Institute, 1996), 19.

8. Martin E.P. Seligman, *The Optimistic Child* (Boston: Houghton Mifflin, 1995).

Getting Started

WITH ASSET BUILDING

Every church is different. Your size, faith tradition, location, congregational priorities, history, and many other factors shape your ministry. So there is no proven, step-by-step formula for integrating asset building into all areas of congregational life.

But there are some concrete ways to get started. This chapter outlines ten steps that lay a foundation for asset-building action and changed attitudes toward young people in your church. Keep in mind that these steps and their order may not fit every congregation. For example, a small congregation may be able to take many of these steps informally, whereas a large congregation may need a more formal process.

STEP #1:

Walk the Talk

Asset building doesn't start with a major program, new curriculum, or endorsement by the church board. It starts with people who commit to doing what they can to ensure that young people have as many asset-building opportunities as possible. So it begins with a personal commitment—your personal commitment.

What can you do to help young people experience more assets? Maybe you start by asking young people to work with you in planning the next mission trip. Maybe you become a mentor for a young person in the congregation or community. Maybe you include examples from school in your next sermon. Or maybe you resign from one of several church committees so you can be home more often with your own children. Whatever it is, identify something that you can and will do to build assets, regardless of whether others in your church get involved.

STEP #2:

Create a Buzz

A second important step is to tell others about asset building, their potential as asset builders, and the possibilities that asset building offers your church. This step works best when you can blend your personal commitment with a solid understanding of the developmental assets and a sense of how this approach might fit with your church's current realities. The goal here is to begin to gauge interest and create a buzz about asset building—a groundswell of interest, momentum, and support.

Who do you talk to first? Depending on your own role and how things happen in your church, begin talking informally with children and youth, parents, church leaders, people who work with children, youth and families, and others in the church with a heart for young people.

As you're sharing your dreams and ideas, keep in mind that people have different natural reactions to innovation and change. Some folks like every new idea; others don't like any new idea! Some folks will only buy in when they know key people they respect are on board. As much as possible, focus energy on finding allies who are open to new ideas and eager to see something happen. There will be time later to draw others into the vision.

STEP #3:

Form an Asset-Building Team

Once you have determined that there is real interest in making asset building part of your church, form a group to think and plan how to integrate asset building more formally into the congregation's programs, activities, and priorities. Identify or assemble a vision team. There are three R's for building a vision team: roles, representation, and respect.

1. Roles focus on what each person will contribute to the asset-building team. A team that seeks to introduce change into a congregation is most effective when it includes people who fill the following roles:

Visionary—Someone who can help the congregation see the potential of asset building and who can ensure that planning is consistent with that vision.

Stakeholder—Someone for whom this idea is critically important. Some key stakeholders are children, youth and parents.

Decision maker—Someone who knows how to get decisions made.

Networker—Someone who is respected and good at building support for ideas by networking and relationship-building.

Manager—Someone who can keep the group on task.

2. Representation focuses on the need to have people connected to many parts of your church involved in the planning group so that many voices and perspectives are heard and taken seriously. Include a cross section of members from young people through senior citizens, from infrequent attenders to congregational leaders. Include people with responsibility for specific areas of congregational life that are particularly relevant for asset building, such as children's ministry, youth ministry, education, community outreach, and fellowship activities.

It's important to have young people involved in planning your asset-building efforts. Indeed, including them on the vision team is a great start for helping them feel valued (asset #7) and for being resources (asset #8).

3. Respect highlights the importance of having people in the group who have credibility and clout in the church. They're people who others look up to for endorsement and approval. They can include church staff, but they also include influential lay people. In most churches, the pastor must be an active supporter—or even initiator—of the asset-building effort. Otherwise it will never gain much support from others. Having the pastor's open support may well be the most important factor in helping your asset-building effort be accepted.

AN ASSET-BUILDING CHURCH

An Open Door After School

Every Monday afternoon, adult mentors are on hand at First United Methodist Church in Albuquerque, New Mexico, as the church opens its door to children from the local middle school for recreation, homework help, and movies.

Also in the works is the Longfellow Publishing Company, where elementary-age children will write, illustrate, and bind their own books; and a bicycle club, where children will learn basic bicycle repair.

Janice Goodjoin of the church says that asset building caught on in her congregation through education. The pastor spoke of asset building in sermons. Goodjoin discussed them with groups in the church and wrote about assets in the church newsletter. Teenagers have created youth outreach efforts that have increased youth participation in worship services. Asset building is slowing transforming their church.

STEP #4:

Listen and Learn

Once a vision team is together, the first task is not to talk but to listen. Your effectiveness in engaging people and structures in the congregation in asset building will depend largely on how well you understand their perspectives, dreams, concerns, and capacities. Without listening first, you are likely to design strategies that will have little "buy-in" from the people who are most affected.

Gathering input and information is an essential part of developing your congregation's asset-building plan. This information can be gathered in a variety of different ways, depending on how precise you want the findings to be and how much energy you can put into the process. But what's important is to take the time to learn from people in your congregation and to listen to their suggestions and feedback.

STEP #5:

Develop a Vision for Asset Building

Once you have a sense of current reality and some priorities for the congregation, begin shaping how you want asset building to look in your congregation. Focus on the kind of congregation you hope to become.

One way of creating a vision is to ask the people who have been reflecting on the information you gathered to each write down what they would hope their congregation would be like in five years if you began an asset-building initiative right now. Encourage them to be concrete and specific. Then gather all these individual vision statements and compile them into themes. Often you will find that five or six themes emerge consistently. These can be reviewed, revised, and ranked in priority to ensure that they capture the spirit and priorities of the congregation. Then they can be used as a focus for planning.

STEP #6:

Shape Your Asset-Building Messages

Commitment will begin to form when individuals see that the congregation's asset emphasis is "about me." If you want individuals (leaders, senior citizens, young adults, and youth) to become active asset builders, focus your specific asset-building themes to their particular needs, hopes, priorities, interests, and gifts.

One important point: You'll be most likely to shape messages that "hit home" if you involve people from the targeted group in developing the message. For example, if you want all adults in the congregation to take time to notice children and youth, get some adults who don't work with young people to help shape the messages and strategies.

STEP #7:

Generate Awareness, Energy, and Commitment

Before your congregation can become committed to asset building, leaders and members need a basic understanding of the idea and motivation to commit themselves to it. The goal at first, then, is to introduce the ideas in ways that spark interest. Then you solidify commitment by involving them in low-risk convenient ways, celebrating early successes, and making it "socially desirable" to build assets.

- Introduce the assets. Focus on ways individuals can be asset builders even without a special program or training. Use the reproducible handouts found on pages 134-147 to distribute to all adults, parents, children, and youth. Share the list of assets and have groups brainstorm about how this approach fits with your congregation's philosophy and theology as well as ways your congregation currently can and does build assets in youth.[1] The "Ideas to Create Awareness About Asset Building" box has more ideas.

When talking with committees and planning groups in the church, focus on the potential of asset building for their areas of responsibility. Make photocopies of reproducible handouts found on pages 148-151 to distribute. There are handouts for worship, fellowship activities, congregational care, and

Ideas to Create Awareness

Use these ideas to publicize asset building in your congregation.

☐ **Newsletters, bulletins, and bulletin boards**—Explain your congregation's commitment, and give ideas of how people can get involved. Publish the information in your worship bulletin or your church newsletter. Tell how individual members are building assets.

☐ **Announcements**—Include the asset-building language when talking about appropriate activities and opportunities in the congregation. Periodically have an Asset-Building Minute in which a congregational member tells about what he or she (or someone else) is doing to build assets. Occasionally have someone remind members what they can do to build assets. For example, say, "Before you leave today, I hope every adult will take an opportunity to greet at least three young people, and every young person will say hi to at least three adults."

☐ **Worship services**—Work with worship leaders to include information about asset building in the worship service through special presentations, liturgical responses, music, or sermons. In some traditions, it may be appropriate to design a complete worship service around the asset-building theme. An opportunity for this is Children's Sabbath in October.

☐ **Special events and celebrations**—Plan a special party, picnic, fair, or other event that highlights asset building. Have banners, balloons, and intergenerational activities that highlight asset building. Or integrate an asset-building focus into an ongoing event in the congregation, such as an annual picnic or banquet.

☐ **Christian education for both youth and adults**—Introduce asset building in educational settings for both youth and adults.

☐ **Presentations to small groups**—There may be a variety of small groups and committees that meet in the congregation, such as women's circles and men's groups, where you could share an asset-building message. You might work with several young people to develop a skit to use with these different groups. After the presentation, have people brainstorm about how their group does or could build assets.

☐ **Congregation's marquee**—If your congregation has a marquee sign on the street, display simple asset-building messages on it.

☐ **Individual conversations**—Never underestimate the power of one-to-one conversations. Have everyone who is committed to asset building talk to at least two other people about it.

☐ **Electronic communication**—Many congregations are now developing web pages and electronic mail. Use these vehicles to communicate about asset building. If your congregation has a Web page, connect it to Search Institute's Web page on asset building, www.search-institute.org.

Integrating Assets
INTO YOUR CONGREGATION

Asset building is about all areas of the congregation, including children and youth in decision making, planning, and doing ministry. Use this work sheet as a way to identify ways children and youth can be involved in these vital ministry areas of your congregation.

AREA	CHILDREN	YOUTH
Worship		
Christian Education		
Congregational Care and Support		
Facilities Maintenance and Operations		
Service		
Social Activities		

An Asset Builder's Pledge

Everyone in our congregation can make a difference in the lives of children and youth. It can begin with a personal commitment to asset building. This asset-building pledge gives concrete ways you can make a difference in the lives of children and youth—whether you're a child, a teenager, or an adult. Please consider signing this pledge. Then, most important, find ways to live the commitment through the coming year.

An Asset Builder's Pledge

In my congregation, community, and world,
I pledge to be an asset builder for children and youth by

A— Advocating

S— Spending time

S— Showing that I care

E— Encouraging and valuing

T— Teaching and mentoring

Each of these commitments can contribute in an important way toward raising healthy, responsible, and caring young people in our congregation. Throughout the year, the Asset-Building Team will provide reminders and tips to help you keep your commitment.

_____   _____   _____
Your full name (printed)   Your signature   Today's date

facilities maintenance and operations. In addition, the worship committee and the music ministry of your church may be interested in the asset-building songs and hymns reproducible handout that appears on pages 152-153. Use the "Integrating Assets Into Your Congregation" work sheet to help brainstorm some of the ways children and youth can be involved in various parts of church life.

● **Provide low-risk opportunities for involvement.** As people are first getting involved, it may be tempting to ask them to jump into the deep end with, for example, a long-term mentoring relationship. Certainly some people are daring and will do it. Most, however, prefer to start in the shallow end with less daunting involvement. To ensure early success, develop and promote opportunities for building assets that are easy and convenient, low cost, and likely to succeed.

● **Apply positive social pressure.** An important way to raise awareness and build commitment is to have influential people in the church advocate for asset-building involvement. Have the pastor speak about asset building during worship services and in other settings. Have the church board endorse asset building and commit themselves to it individually. In our congregation, we created an asset builders' pledge (p. 123) and invited people to make a public commitment to building assets.

STEP #8:

Set Up Systems for Success

Getting people interested and committed is only half of the equation. Your efforts will only have a long-term impact if you establish systems that support, strengthen, deepen, and renew people's commitment.

● **Deepen leaders' understanding of asset building.** Challenge yourself and your planning team to become experts in asset building. Start with what you know. But as you gain experience and questions arise, dig deeper. Learn more about the assets and how they apply to congregations. Appendix 2 (p. 155) suggests additional resources. New information and opportunities for growth and learning can also be found at Search Institute's Web site: www.search-institute.org.

● **Educate people about asset building.** Part of the challenge is to keep the message fresh and visible. In addition, new people who enter the congregation need to learn about it. So the awareness raising never really ends. More important, though, people need opportunities to move beyond awareness to deeper knowledge and personal reflection about assets and their role as asset builders. Consider providing classes or workshops on asset building for interested church members.[2] Develop parenting classes using the assets as a

starting point. Focus on the assets in youth group meetings, Christian education classes, or retreats.[3]

● **Teach specific skills for asset building.** One reason some adults don't talk with youth is that they don't really know how. Christian education leaders may not have the skills they need to nurture positive values in young people. Or parents may struggle with how to set appropriate boundaries. Therefore, in addition to education to deepen their understanding of asset building, people need opportunities to be trained as asset builders. This involves identifying (by asking) areas where people feel inadequate, then providing very concrete help and practice in the skills that increase their comfort levels in those areas.

● **Provide opportunities for people to practice asset building.** Education and training are not enough. They need to be coupled with concrete opportunities for the people in the congregation to practice and live out their commitment to asset building. At St. Luke Presbyterian Church, we lead a one-week intergenerational class. Instead of developing a lot of material, we created a discussion-starter game. Participants drew cards that had questions related to one of the eight categories of assets. The questions were about people's experiences, their beliefs, funny stories—many different

Assessing Activities

THROUGH AN ASSET-BUILDING LENS

In order to continually increase the asset-building strength of programs and activities in your church, take time to debrief or reflect on activities using the eight categories of developmental assets. Complete this work sheet after an event, then refer to it the next time you plan a similar activity.

Activity Description: _____ Date: _____

Asset Category	How the Activity Built These Assets	Other Ways It Could Build These Assets
Support: How did the activity reinforce caring relationships and a warm climate in which all young people felt welcomed and accepted?		
Empowerment: How did the activity empower young people to serve and lead? How well did it offer physical and emotional safety?		
Boundaries and Expectations: How did the activity support appropriate boundaries for behavior? How did it challenge young people to be their best?		
Constructive Use of Time: How did the activity use young people's time for enrichment and growth?		
Commitment to Learning: How did the activity reinforce curiosity, learning, and discovery?		
Positive Values: How did the activity reinforce and articulate positive values?		
Social Competencies: How did the activity build young people's life and relationship skills?		
Positive Identity: How did the activity nurture in young people a sense of purpose, value, and possibility?		

AN ASSET-BUILDING CONGREGATION

Reaching Out to the Community

Who we are is just one piece of the pie," says Nancy Going, director of youth and family ministry at Trinity Lutheran Church in Town and Country, Missouri. So far, the rest of the pie in this suburb of St. Louis consists of the school district, police department, and hospital leaders, who together want to make a difference in the lives of youth. And the pie is growing!

Trinity originally introduced the asset-building framework to Parkway School District, which, in turn, planned an educational meeting for clergy, hospital personnel, business and industry leaders, and others. These meetings led to a survey of youth to get a handle on what their youth needed.

Rob Rose, former senior high youth minister at Trinity, believes the congregation is at the heart of the initiative. "Part of our church's philosophy is that Trinity needs to be a community center. We need to be more than just a building. We need to go out into the community and work in the community to make it better. That's what we're doing with assets."

things that not only taught a bit about asset building, but also helped people start talking to each other and learn about each other's lives. In the process, they learned it wasn't as hard as they thought to talk to people from other generations.

- **Recognize people for their asset-building efforts.** One way to reinforce people's commitment and involvement is to publicly recognize and affirm their efforts. An "Asset Builder of the Month" column in your newsletter, an asset builder's picnic, and recognition during a worship service are just a few forms of affirmation that can celebrate both an individual's commitment to asset building as well as the whole congregation's.

- **Monitor and evaluate your efforts.** Finally, the long-term success of your asset-building efforts can be greatly enhanced if you keep track of how things are going and reshape your work when you detect rough spots. Not only is it important to check to see if people are actually getting involved, but also to see if those experiences have been positive and rewarding for everyone. If so, you have something to celebrate. If not, you can work to improve the system before too many people get discouraged or disillusioned.

STEP #9:

Infuse Asset Building Into Programs and Activities

Asset building can clearly be used to strengthen many programmatic areas of your church. What would children's Sunday school look like if you used the assets as a foundation for planning? How do you involve parents? How would you help children feel valued by giving them appropriate roles and responsibilities in the class? The list of questions could go on, addressing each of the eight categories of assets.

Several common youth programs have great potential for asset building, including peer ministry, music, youth leadership, sports, and community service or missions. These activities probably already do a lot to build assets. How might a focus on the assets help you strengthen these existing efforts? The "Assessing Activities Through an Asset-Building Lens" work sheet provides a tool for evaluating existing efforts and exploring how to strengthen them from an asset perspective.[4]

STEP #10:

Network With Others

One of the key messages of asset building is that everyone and all sectors in a community can play a role in building assets. Knowing you are part of a larger effort can bring energy and enthusiasm to your congregation's work. Here are some ways to network in your community:

● Partner with other pastors, Christian education leaders, and youth workers for support, ideas, problem-solving skills, and renewal.

● Work with other congregations to sponsor joint programs or training that your congregation could not do alone.

● Build connections with other organizations in your community that are committed to asset building. These may include schools, health care providers, youth organizations, social service agencies, and parks and recreation organizations.

● Find out if there is already a multisector asset-building effort in your community. See how it can be a resource to you—and you a resource to it! (A list of community asset-building initiatives can be found on Search Institute's Web site: www.search-institute.org.)

Your networking can extend beyond your own community as well. Connect with other congrega-

tional leaders in your denomination or informal network who know about and are committed to asset building. Consider attending training events or conferences about asset building so that you can connect with and learn from others.[5]

General Asset-Building Ideas for All Ministries

● Keep asset building as part of congregational staff meetings and congregational board meetings. Discuss the implications that asset building has for your congregation and brainstorm ideas together.

● Lead a series of classes (or preach sermons) that introduce the developmental assets to everyone in the congregation.

● Regularly encourage all members of the congregation to think of themselves as asset builders for young people in their families, congregation, neighborhood, and community.

● Survey the congregation on needs, interests, and priorities related to asset building. Then include a regular report on children's ministry, youth work, and asset building on the congregational board's agenda.

● Make your facility an asset-building place. Rent or provide free space for children and youth clubs to use when your building is typically empty. Host a neighborhood child-care center.

General Asset-Building Ideas for Church Nurseries

● Greet children and parents as they arrive, even if you already have a child in your arms. Make drop-off and pick-up times warm and welcoming.

● Be firm and consistent with the daily schedule. Children feel more secure when they have naps, mealtimes, playtimes, and other activities occurring at the same time each day.

● Tell parents about asset building. Give them the list of forty developmental assets that fit the age of their child. Encourage them to post the list at home.

● Give children simple, age-appropriate activities that encourage their independence and leadership. For example, ask a different toddler to choose a book to have read aloud during group reading times.

● Keep learning about child development and ways to create a stimulating, yet nurturing environment in your church nursery.

AN ASSET-BUILDING CHURCH

Everyone's a Youth Pastor

We have a lot of motivated people who understand that this is not a program," says Father Mark McCormick of St. Anthony's of Padua in Hot Springs, South Dakota. "They've been willing to go beyond just workshops and talk to as many people as they can."

Asset building is slowly changing the parish. "We put three young people on our parish council, but they didn't like the meetings," Father McCormick says. "Instead, we asked them to come for just a half an hour to present ideas on specific topics. This strategy kept one young person from leaving."

St. Anthony's matches some of its senior members with young people unable to attend church regularly to work as educational mentors and just make friends. "Our elders see that they can be youth pastors," McCormick says. Youth also reciprocate. McCormick cites the example of a seventy-two-year-old parishioner who was nervous about serving mass for the first time. A young person offered reassurance, which provided confidence and composure.

General Asset-Building Ideas for Children's Ministry

● Relate in positive, meaningful ways with children in your ministry, and encourage volunteers in your ministry to also do so. Find out more about childhood development and the forty developmental assets that focus on the age of children within your ministry. There are four lists of developmental assets for children: one for infants (birth to twelve months), one for toddlers (thirteen to thirty-five months), one for preschoolers (ages three to five), and one for elementary-age children (ages six to eleven).

● Be concrete and explicit about teaching children practical skills, such as peaceful conflict resolution (asset #36), resistance skills (asset #35), and planning and decision-making skills (asset #32).

● Find books and videos that tie into asset building. For example, *I Wanted to Know All About God* by Virginia L. Kroll (Grand Rapids, MI: William B. Eerdmans, 1994) ties into many of the forty assets. *Old Turtle* by Douglas Wood (Duluth, MN: Pfeifer-Hamilton, 1992) promotes our relationship with God and with everyone on earth, which emphasizes the assets of support and positive values. The video series based on *The Book of Virtues* by William Bennett (Los Angeles: KCET/Los Angeles and Porchlight Entertainment, 1996) also focuses on specific assets, such as the video on friendship (assets #15 and #33), compassion (asset #26), honesty (asset #29), and responsibility (asset #30).

● Keep ground rules simple and clear. As a group, discuss boundaries and what the consequences are.

● Create a caring climate within your group. When children come, make eye contact with them. Smile. Show them how happy you are to see them, even if your enthusiasm is running low.

General Asset-Building Ideas for Youth Ministry

● Tell young people about assets and see what they think. Consider leading activities that introduce the assets to youth. For example, *Building Assets Together* by Jolene L. Roehlkepartain (Minneapolis: Search Institute, 1997) offers group activities and reproducible work sheets to introduce each of the forty assets to teenagers.

● Involve youth in planning and leading youth activities and programs.

● Form an asset-building team and work through *Strategic Youth Ministry* together (Loveland, CO: Group, 2000).

● Engage people from many backgrounds and generations as youth program volunteers so young people have opportunities to build relationships with many generations.

- Assess all your youth programming through an asset-building lens. What are the ways your youth ministry already builds many assets? What could be done to touch on even more of the assets?

- Ensure that retreats, camps, and trips are asset-building experiences. Balance fun with learning, and encourage relationships to build. Take time after these experiences to reflect on what happened—the positives and the negatives—to help young people process what they learned.

General Asset-Building Ideas for Family Ministry

- Get to know the families of children and teenagers—not just their names—but their interests, needs, and realities. This will send an important signal that you are there to serve and support them, not to coax them into taking on yet another responsibility in the congregation.

- Offer parent and teenagers workshops on asset-building topics, such as family support (asset #1) and resistance skills (asset #35).

- Address family issues in sermons, and include take-home discussion starters in the worship bulletin.

- Lobby for public and corporate policies that make it easier for families to build assets.

- Encourage families to develop a family mission statement that focuses on building assets. Have families use this statement as a guide for family decisions and priorities.

General Asset-Building Ideas for Christian Education

- Focus special seminars or workshops on asset building.

- Involve youth on the educational leadership committee or team.

- Recruit youth as leaders or assistants for children's education.

- Offer adult classes in which adults learn about developmental assets and their connection to your faith tradition's theology and practice.

- Offer classes to help individuals build skills for asset building, such as relationship skills and advocacy skills.

General Asset-Building Ideas for Intergenerational Ministry

- Do an audit of the congregation-wide activities you offer. Are children and youth welcomed and included? Find places where you can be more intentional about intergenerational community.

- Train older people in your congregation to become elders or grandparents for children and teenagers in the congregation.

Discuss the important role that older people have in the lives of young people.

- Find mutually enjoyable ways to match the generations for growth and learning, such as creating intergenerational theater groups, choruses, retreats, and board game competitions.

- Encourage people of all ages to give spontaneous gestures of support to children and youth in your congregation. These are simple, easy interactions, such as calling young people by name, smiling at them, and asking them about their day.

- Create programs that encourage intergenerational relationships through mentoring programs. Carefully match a caring adult with a young person and encourage them to build a relationship.

General Asset-Building Ideas for Community Outreach

- Coordinate your asset-building efforts with other congregations. Offer each other ideas and support.

- Sponsor billboards or other public service announcements related to asset building. Highlight the positive ways people can interact with children and youth and what young people contribute to the community.

- Join with (or start) a community-wide partnership for asset building. (To see if your community has an existing initiative, check the listing on Search Institute's Web site at www.search-institute.org.)

● Identify members of your congregation who are already involved in community leadership roles. Encourage them to be champions of asset building through their existing responsibilities.

● Many members of your congregation are already active volunteers in community-based organizations. One way to extend your reach into the community is to identify, encourage, and celebrate members' involvement.

NOTES

1. Ready-to-use outlines and reproducible handouts and transparencies for five workshop-style presentations on asset building in congregations are available in Jolene L. Roehlkepartain and James Conway, *Get on Board! Presentations and Activities for Introducing Asset Building in Congregations* (Minneapolis: Search Institute, 1999).

2. A tool that's useful in adult education settings is *Taking Asset Building Personally* (Minneapolis: Search Institute, 1999). It includes outlines for six small-group sessions and a personal action guide that helps participants examine how they can build assets.

3. A tool with activities and work sheets for youth on each of the forty assets is Jolene L. Roehlkepartain, *Building Assets Together: 135 Group Activities or Helping Youth Succeed*

(Minneapolis: Search Institute, 1997).

4. Search Institute has developed asset builder's guides to several programming areas that are relevant for churches. They include *An Asset Builder's Guide to Youth Leadership; An Asset Builder's Guide to Service-Learning;* and *An Asset Builder's Guide to Youth and Money,* which is valuable for stewardship education. Each shows how to make asset building part of these programs.

5. Each fall Search Institute sponsors a national Healthy Communities • Healthy Youth Conference, which includes several learning sessions for congregations. Several state networks have begun to form as well, and they also sponsor their own conferences. Updated information is available on Search Institute's Web site: www.search-institute.org.

Making Common Sense Common Again

Derek Peterson and Becky Judd are asset-building champions in the state of Alaska. Through work in statewide organizations, they have planted asset-building seeds in hundreds of cities, towns, and villages throughout the state—some of which are accessible only by boat or plane. Because they are aware of the vast cultural differences across the state (and in comparison to "the lower forty-eight"), Peterson and Judd are careful to listen and learn wherever they go.

Once during a presentation in a remote village with about six hundred residents, Peterson noticed a village elder sitting in the back of the room. For about forty minutes, Peterson presented the assets and the research behind them. He asked people to share their ideas for how to build the assets.

The elder stood up. "For years," he said, "we have been telling people that we need to focus on the strengths of our communities, the strengths of our traditions, and the strengths of ourselves. These are the things that we focused on a long time ago, and we've been waiting seventy-five years for these things to be focused on again."[1]

That elder was right. The assets themselves really aren't new. Many people, families, institutions, and cultures have been building assets for centuries. They're not really anything new.

We've just forgotten how important these strengths are.

The same could be said in churches. Churches have been doing things that build assets for as long as they've been

around. You could probably find most of the ideas in this book in other resources for children, youth, and family ministry. Many of them are entirely consistent with principles of effective ministry. The language is a little different, and it's not organized the same way churches typically organize their ministries. But it's a lot of the same stuff.

That said, sometimes we overlook the most obvious things. Sometimes we forget how important these things are. Sometimes we need to be reminded of the essentials.

Since Search Institute's framework of developmental assets was first developed in 1990, it has become a valuable tool and resource for individuals, families, organizations, and communities to understand what's happening with youth in this society and what they need to succeed. For many people, the assets have become a reminder that, as another Alaskan elder concluded, "common sense isn't so common anymore."

The assets—and the research behind them—remind us of the strengths and resources we have to offer our kids in our homes, churches, schools, families, and communities. They remind us that what we do each and every day and how we relate to children and teenagers week after week can have a profound and important influence on their lives.

Are these new ideas? Not really. But the new framework and the research behind it offer a fresh perspective on ministry. They also remind us how fragile these forty assets are for most young people. The task is not just important—it's urgent. Assets remind us of the tremendous potential we have in our churches to make a difference for chil-

dren and youth—not just in our congregations, but in our communities as well.

Though asset-building efforts in churches often begin small and in seemingly inconsequential ways, the long-term potential is tremendous. Individual acts and commitments add up. Programming changes can raise the enthusiasm of young people. Empowering children and youth gives a sense of accomplishment. Piece by piece, these positive experiences build on each other to rebuild a solid foundation for life.

In Search Institute's work in networking congregations for asset building, one of the metaphors that was often used was the story of stone soup. It's the story of a village where no one had the needed ingredients to make soup, so all were going hungry. A stranger came to town and announced that he would make stone soup. The villagers watched with curiosity.

As the water heated, the stranger would remark, "This soup would be so much better if it had a bit of onion." And someone would then remember an onion in the pantry. Then some spices, some broth, some vegetables would be added. Before long, the villagers had created a wonderful soup based on what they each brought.

That's how asset building works. No one person or church or family can build all the assets a young person needs. But if we all offer what we have been given, then the results in the lives of children and youth will be amazing!

NOTES

1. *Helping Kids Succeed—Alaskan Style* (Juneau, AK: Association of Alaska School Boards, 1998), 21. Distributed by Search Institute.

Reproducible Handouts

APPENDIX 1

40 Developmental Assets for Infants

BIRTH TO TWELVE MONTHS

SEARCH INSTITUTE *has identified a framework of forty developmental assets for infants from birth to age one that blends* SEARCH INSTITUTE'S *research on developmental assets for twelve- to eighteen-year-olds with the extensive literature on child development.*

ASSET TYPE	ASSET NAME AND DEFINITION
Support	**1. Family Support**—Family life provides high levels of love and support.
	2. Positive family communication—Parent(s) communicate with the infant in positive ways. Parent(s) respond immediately to the infant and respect the infant's needs.
	3. Other adult resources—Parent(s) receive support from three or more nonparent adults and ask for help when needed. The infant receives additional love and comfort from at least one nonparent adult.
	4. Caring neighborhood—Infant experiences caring neighbors.
	5. Caring out-of-home climate—Infant is in caring, encouraging environments outside the home.
	6. Parent involvement in out-of-home situations—Parent(s) are actively involved in communicating the infant's needs to caretakers and in other situations or experiences outside the home.
Empowerment	**7. Children valued**—The family places the infant at the center of family life. Other adults in the community value and appreciate infants.
	8. Child has role in family life—The family involves the infant in family life.
	9. Service to others—Parent(s) serve others in the community.
	10. Safety—Infant has a safe environment at home, in out-of-home settings, and in the neighborhood. This includes, but is not limited to, child proofing these environments as the infant begins to explore her or his environment.
Boundaries & Expectations	**11. Family boundaries**—Parent(s) are aware of the infant's preferences and adapt the environment and schedule to best suit the infant's needs. Parent(s) begin setting limits as the infant becomes mobile.
	12. Out-of-home boundaries—Child care and other out-of-home environments have clear rules and consequences for older infants while consistently providing all infants with appropriate stimulation and enough rest.
	13. Neighborhood boundaries—Neighbors take responsibility for monitoring the infant's behavior as the infant begins to play and interact outside the home.
	14. Adult role models—Parent(s) and other adults model positive, responsible behavior.
	15. Positive peer observation—Infant observes positive peer interactions of siblings and other children and has opportunities for beginning interactions with other children of various ages.
	16. Expectations for growth—Parent(s) are realistic in their expectations of development at this age. Parent(s) encourage development but do not push the infant beyond her or his own pace.
Constructive Use of Time	**17. Creative activities**—Parent(s) daily expose the infant to music, art, or other creative aspects of the environment.
	18. Out-of-home activities—Parent(s) expose the infant to limited but stimulating situations outside of the home. Family attends events with the infant's needs in mind.
	19. Religious community—Family attends religious activities or services on a regular basis while keeping the infant's needs in mind.
	20. Positive, supervised time at home—Parent(s) supervise the infant at all times and provide predictable and enjoyable routines at home.

ASSET TYPE	ASSET NAME AND DEFINITION
Commitment to Learning	21. **Achievement expectation**—Family members are motivated to do well at work, school, and in the community, which serves as a beginning of modeling this motivation to the infant.
	22. **Engagement expectation**—The family models responsive and attentive attitudes at work, school, in the community, and at home.
	23. **Stimulating activity**—Parent(s) encourage the infant to explore and provide stimulating toys that match the infant's emerging skills. Parent(s) are sensitive to the infant's level of development, disposition, and tolerance for movement, sounds, and duration of activity.
	24. **Enjoyment of learning**—Parent(s) enjoy learning and begin to model this through their own learning activities.
	25. **Reading for pleasure**—Parent(s) read to the infant daily in enjoyable ways.
Positive Values	26. **Family values caring**—Parent(s) convey their beliefs about helping others by beginning to model their helping behaviors.
	27. **Family values equality and social justice**—Parent(s) place a high value on promoting social equality, religious tolerance, and reducing hunger and poverty, while modeling these beliefs.
	28. **Family values integrity**—Parent(s) act on convictions and stand up for their beliefs and begin to communicate and model this in the family.
	29. **Family values honesty**—Parent(s) tell the truth and convey their belief in honesty through their actions.
	30. **Family values responsibility**—Parent(s) accept and take personal responsibility.
	31. **Family values a healthy lifestyle and sexual attitudes**—Parent(s) love the infant, setting the foundation for the infant to develop healthy attitudes and beliefs about relationships. Parent(s) begin to model, monitor, and teach the importance of good health habits, such as providing good nutritional choices and adequate rest and playtime.
Social Competencies	32. **Planning and decision-making observation**—Parent(s) make all safety and care decisions for the infant and begin to model these behaviors. Parent(s) allow the infant to make simple choices as the infant becomes more independently mobile.
	33. **Interpersonal observation**—Parent(s) begin to model positive and constructive interactions with other people. Parent(s) accept and are responsive to the infant's expression of feelings, interpreting those expressions as cues to the infant's needs.
	34. **Cultural observation**—Parent(s) have knowledge of and are comfortable with people of different cultural/racial/ethnic backgrounds and begin to model this to the infant.
	35. **Resistance observation**—Parent(s) begin to model resistance skills through their own behaviors.
	36. **Peaceful conflict resolution observation**—Parent(s) behave in acceptable, nonviolent ways and assist the infant in developing these skills when faced with challenging or frustrating circumstances by beginning to help the infant solve problems.
Positive Identity	37. **Family has personal power**—Parent(s) feel they have control over things that happen to them and model coping skills, demonstrating healthy ways to deal with frustrations and challenges. Parent(s) are responsive to the infant and the infant begins to learn that he or she can influence her or his immediate surroundings.
	38. **Family models high self-esteem**—Parent(s) create an environment where the infant can develop positive self-esteem, giving the infant appropriate positive feedback and reinforcement about emerging skills and competencies.
	39. **Family has a sense of purpose**—Parent(s) report that their lives have purpose and demonstrate these beliefs through their behaviors. Infant demonstrates curiosity in the world around her or him.
	40. **Family has a positive view of the future**—Parent(s) are hopeful and positive about their personal future and work to provide a positive future for the infant.

40 Developmental Assets for Toddlers

THIRTEEN MONTHS TO THIRTY-FIVE MONTHS

SEARCH INSTITUTE *has identified a framework of forty developmental assets for toddlers from thirteen to thirty-five months that blends* SEARCH INSTITUTE'S *research on developmental assets for twelve- to eighteen-year-olds with the extensive literature in child development.*

ASSET TYPE	ASSET NAME AND DEFINITION
Support	**1. Family support**—Family life provides high levels of love and support.
	2. Positive family communicaion—Parent(s) communicate with the toddler in positive ways. Parent(s) respond to the toddler's needs and respect those needs.
	3. Other adult resources—Parent(s) receive support from three or more nonparent adults and ask for help when needed. The toddler receives additional love and comfort from at least one nonparent adult.
	4. Caring neighborhood—Toddler experiences caring neighbors.
	5. Caring out-of-home climate—Toddler is in caring, encouraging environments outside the home.
	6. Parent involvement in out-of-home situations—Parent(s) are actively involved in helping the toddler succeed in situations outside the home and communicate the toddler's developmental needs to caretakers outside the home.
Empowerment	**7. Children valued**—The family places the toddler at the center of family life and also recognizes the need for limit setting with the toddler. Other adults in the community value and appreciate toddlers.
	8. Child has role in family life—The family involves the toddler in family life.
	9. Service to others—Parent(s) serve others in the community.
	10. Safety—Toddler has a safe environment at home, in out-of-home settings, and in the neighborhood, which includes child proofing these environments.
Boundaries & Expectations	**11. Family boundaries**—Parent(s) are aware of the toddler's preferences and adapt the environment to best suit the toddler's needs. Parent(s) set age-appropriate limits for the toddler.
	12. Out-of-home boundaries—Child care and other out-of-home environments have clear rules and consequences, which protect the toddler, while consistently providing the toddler with appropriate stimulation and enough rest.
	13. Neighborhood boundaries—Neighbors take responsibility for supervising and monitoring the toddler's behavior as the toddler begins to play and interact outside the home.
	14. Adult role models—Parent(s) and other adults model positive, responsible behavior.
	15. Positive peer observation—Toddler observes positive peer interactions of siblings and other children and has opportunities for interactions with children of various ages.
	16. Expectations for growth—Parent(s) are realistic in their expectations of development at this age. Parent(s) encourage development but do not push the toddler beyond her or his own pace.
Constructive Use of Time	**17. Creative activities**—Parent(s) daily expose the toddler to music, art, or other creative age-appropriate activities.
	18. Out-of-home activities—Parent(s) expose the toddler to limited but stimulating situations outside of the home. Family attends events with the toddler's needs in mind.
	19. Religious community—Family attends religious programs or services on a regular basis while keeping the toddler's needs in mind.
	20. Positive, supervised time at home—Parent(s) supervise the toddler at all times and provide predictable and enjoyable routines at home.

ASSET TYPE	ASSET NAME AND DEFINITION
Commitment to Learning	**21. Achievement expectation**—Family members are motivated to do well at work, school, and in the community and model this motivation to the toddler.
	22. Engagement expectation—The family models responsive and attentive attitudes at work, school, in the community, and at home.
	23. Stimulating activity—Parent(s) encourage the toddler to explore, and they provide stimulating toys that match the toddler's emerging skills. Parent(s) are sensitive to the toddler's level of development and tolerance for movement, sounds, and duration of activity.
	24. Enjoyment of learning—Parent(s) enjoy learning, and demonstrate this through their own learning activities.
	25. Reading for pleasure—Parent(s) read to the toddler daily in ways that allow the toddler to participate in reading experiences, such as turning pages and identifying characters or animals in books.
Positive Values	**26. Family values caring**—Parent(s) convey their beliefs about helping others through modeling their helping behaviors.
	27. Family values equality and social justice—Parent(s) place a high value on promoting social equality, religious tolerance, and reducing hunger and poverty while modeling these beliefs.
	28. Family values integrity—Parent(s) act on convictions and stand up for their beliefs and communicate and model this in the family.
	29. Family values honesty—Parent(s) tell the truth and convey their belief in honesty through their actions.
	30. Family values responsibility—Parent(s) accept and take personal responsibility.
	31. Family values a healthy lifestyle and sexual attitudes—Parent(s) love the toddler, setting the foundation for the toddler to develop healthy attitudes and beliefs about relationships. Parent(s) model, monitor, and teach the importance of good health habits, such as providing good nutritional choices and adequate rest and playtime.
Social Competencies	**32. Planning and decision-making observation**—Parent(s) make all safety and care decisions for the toddler and then model these behaviors. Parent(s) allow the toddler to make simple choices as the toddler becomes more independently mobile.
	33. Interpersonal observation—Parent(s) model positive and constructive interactions with other people. Parent(s) accept and are responsive to the toddler's expression of feelings through actions and beginning language skills, interpreting those expressions as cues of the toddler's needs.
	34. Cultural observation—Parent(s) have knowledge of and are comfortable with people of different cultural/racial/ethnic backgrounds and model this to the toddler.
	35. Resistance observation—Parent(s) model resistance skills through their own behaviors.
	36. Peaceful conflict resolution observation—Parent(s) behave in acceptable, nonviolent ways and assist the toddler to develop these skills when faced with challenging or frustrating circumstances by helping the toddler learn to solve problems.
Positive Identity	**37. Family has personal power**—Parent(s) feel they have control over things that happen to them and model coping skills, demonstrating healthy ways to deal with frustrations and challenges. Parent(s) are responsive to the toddler and the toddler begins to learn that he or she can influence her or his immediate surroundings.
	38. Family models high self-esteem—Parent(s) model high self-esteem and create an environment where the toddler can develop positive self-esteem, giving the toddler appropriate positive feedback and reinforcement about skills and competencies.
	39. Family has a sense of purpose—Parent(s) report that their lives have purpose and model these beliefs through their behaviors. The toddler demonstrates curiosity in and exploration of the world around her or him.
	40. Family has a positive view of the future—Parent(s) are hopeful and optimistic about their personal future and work to provide a positive future for the toddler.

40 Developmental Assets for Preschoolers

AGES THREE TO FIVE

SEARCH INSTITUTE *has identified a framework of forty developmental assets for children ages three to five that blends* SEARCH INSTITUTE'S *research on developmental assets for twelve- to eighteen-year-olds with the extensive literature in child development.*

ASSET TYPE	ASSET NAME AND DEFINITION
Support	**1. Family support**—Family life provides high levels of love and support.
	2. Positive family communication—Parent(s) and child communicate positively. Child seeks out parent(s) for assistance with difficult tasks or situations.
	3. Other adult resources—Child receives support from at least one nonparent adult. Parent(s) have support from individuals outside the home.
	4. Caring neighborhood—Child experiences caring neighbors.
	5. Caring out-of-home climate—Child is in caring, encouraging environments outside the home.
	6. Parent involvement in out-of-home situations—Parent(s) are actively involved in helping child succeed in situations outside the home.
Empowerment	**7. Children valued**—Parent(s) and other adults in the community value and appreciate children.
	8. Children given useful roles—Parent(s) and other adults create ways the child can help out and gradually include the child in age-appropriate tasks.
	9. Service to others—The family serves others in the community together.
	10. Safety—Child has a safe environment at home, in out-of-home settings, and in the neighborhood.
Boundaries & Expectations	**11. Family boundaries**—Family has clear rules and consequences. Family monitors the child and consistently demonstrates appropriate behavior through modeling and limit setting.
	12. Out-of-home boundaries—Neighbors, child care, preschool, and community provide clear rules and consequences.
	13. Neighborhood boundaries—Neighbors take responsibility for monitoring the child's behavior as the child plays and interacts outside the home.
	14. Adult role models—Parent(s) and other adults model positive, responsible behavior.
	15. Positive peer interactions—Child's interactions with other children are encouraged and promoted. Child is provided opportunities to play and interact with other children in a safe, well-supervised setting.
	16. Expectations for growth—Adults have realistic expectations of development at this age. Parent(s), caregivers, and other adults encourage child to achieve and develop her or his unique talents.
Constructive Use of Time	**17. Creative activities**—Child participates in music, art, or dramatic play on a daily basis.
	18. Out-of-home activities—Child interacts with children outside the family in stimulating situations. Family attends events with the child's needs in mind.
	19. Religious community—Family attends a religious program or service on a regular basis while keeping the child's needs in mind.
	20. Positive, supervised time at home—Child is supervised by an adult at all times. Child spends most evenings and weekends at home with parent(s) in predictable, fun, enjoyable routines.

ASSET TYPE	ASSET NAME AND DEFINITION
Commitment to Learning	21. **Achievement expectation**—Parent(s) and other adults convey and reinforce expectations to do well at work, school, in the community, and within the family. 22. **Engagement expectation**—Parent(s) model responsive and attentive attitudes at work, school, in the community, and at home. 23. **Stimulating activity**—Parent(s) and other adults encourage the child to explore and provide stimulating toys that match the child's emerging skills. Parent(s) and other adults are sensitive to the child's level of development. 24. **Enjoyment of learning**—Parent(s) and other adults enjoy learning and engage the child in learning activities. 25. **Reading for pleasure**—Child is read to by a caring adult for at least thirty minutes a day and is encouraged to participate.
Positive Values	26. **Family values caring**—Child is encouraged to express sympathy for someone who is distressed and begins to develop a variety of helping behaviors. 27. **Family values equality and social justice**—Parent(s) place a high value on promoting social equality, religious tolerance, and reducing hunger and poverty while modeling these beliefs. 28. **Family values integrity**—Parent(s) act on convictions and stand up for their beliefs and communicate and model this in the family. 29. **Family values honesty**—Child learns the difference between truth and lying. 30. **Family values responsibility**—Child learns that actions have an effect on other people. 31. **Family values a healthy lifestyle and sexual attitudes**—Parent(s) and other adults model, monitor, and teach the importance of good health habits. Child begins to learn healthy sexual attitudes and beliefs as well as respect for others.
Social Competencies	32. **Planning and decision-making practice**—Child begins to make simple choices, solve simple problems, and develop simple plans at an age-appropriate level. 33. **Interpersonal interactions**—Child plays and interacts with other children and adults. Child freely expresses feelings and learns to articulate feelings verbally. Parent(s) and other adults model and teach empathy. 34. **Cultural interactions**—Child is positively exposed to information and people of different cultural/racial/ethnic backgrounds. 35. **Resistance practice**—Child is taught to resist participating in behavior that is inappropriate or dangerous. 36. **Peaceful conflict resolution practice**—Parent(s) and other adults model positive ways to resolve conflicts. Child is taught and begins to practice nonviolent, acceptable ways to deal with challenging and frustrating situations.
Positive Identity	37. **Family has personal power**—Parent(s) feel they have control over things that happen to them and model coping skills, demonstrating healthy ways to deal with frustrations and challenges. Parent(s) are responsive to the child and the child begins to learn that he or she can influence her or his immediate surroundings. 38. **Family models high self-esteem**—Parent(s) model high self-esteem and create an environment where the child can develop positive self-esteem, giving the child appropriate positive feedback and reinforcement about skills and competencies. 39. **Family has a sense of purpose**—Parent(s) report that their lives have purpose and model these beliefs through their behaviors. The child demonstrates curiosity in and the exploration of the world around her or him. 40. **Family has a positive view of the future**—Parent(s) are hopeful and positive about their personal future and work to provide a positive future for the child.

40 Developmental Assets for Elementary-Age

CHILDREN AGES SIX TO ELEVEN

SEARCH INSTITUTE *has identified a framework of forty developmental assets for children ages six to eleven that blends* SEARCH INSTITUTE'S *research on developmental assets for twelve- to eighteen-year-olds with the extensive literature in child development.*

ASSET TYPE	ASSET NAME AND DEFINITION
Support	**1. Family support**—Family life provides high levels of love and support.
	2. Positive family communication—Parent(s) and child communicate positively. Child is willing to seek parental advice and counsel.
	3. Other adult relationships—Child receives support from nonparent adults.
	4. Caring neighborhood—Child experiences caring neighbors.
	5. Caring school climate—School and other activities provide caring, encouraging environments.
	6. Parent involvement in schooling—Parent(s) are actively involved in helping child succeed in school.
Empowerment	**7. Community values children**—Children feel that the family and the community values and appreciates children.
	8. Children given useful roles—Child is included in age-appropriate family tasks and decisions and is given useful roles at home and in the community.
	9. Service to others—Child and parent(s) serve others and the community.
	10. Safety—Child is safe at home, at school, and in the neighborhood.
Boundaries & Expectations	**11. Family boundaries**—Family has clear rules and consequences, and monitors the child's activities and whereabouts.
	12. School boundaries—School provides clear rules and consequences.
	13. Neighborhood boundaries—Neighbors take responsibility for monitoring the child's behavior.
	14. Adult role models—Parent(s) and other adults model positive, responsible behavior.
	15. Positive peer interactions—Child interacts with other children who model responsible behavior and has opportunities to play and interact in safe, well-supervised settings.
	16. Expectations for growth—Adults have realistic expectations of development at this age. Parent(s), caregivers, and other adults encourage child to achieve and develop her or his unique talents.
Constructive Use of Time	**17. Creative activities**—Child participates in music, arts, or drama three or more hours each week through home and out-of-home activities.
	18. Child programs—Child spends one hour or more per week in extracurricular school or structured community programs.
	19. Religious community—Family attends religious programs or services for at least one hour once a week.
	20. Positive, supervised time at home—Child spends most evenings and weekends at home with parent(s) in predictable and enjoyable routines.

ASSET TYPE	ASSET NAME AND DEFINITION
Commitment to Learning	**21. Achievement motivation**—Child is motivated to do well in school. **22. School engagement**—Child is responsive, attentive, and actively engaged in learning. **23. Homework**—Child is encouraged by parents and teachers to explore and engage in stimulating activities. Child does homework when it is assigned. **24. Bonding to school**—Child cares about her or his school. **25. Reading for pleasure**—Child and a caring adult read together for at least thirty minutes a day. Child also enjoys reading or looking at books or magazines without an adult's involvement.
Positive Values	**26. Caring**—Child is encouraged to help other people. **27. Equality and social justice**—Child begins to show interest in making the community a better place. **28. Integrity**—Child begins to act on convictions and stand up for her or his beliefs. **29. Honesty**—Child begins to value honesty and act accordingly. **30. Responsibility**—Child begins to accept and take personal responsibility for age-appropriate tasks. **31. Healthy lifestyle and sexual attitudes**—Child begins to value good health habits. Child learns healthy sexual attitudes and beliefs as well as respect for others.
Social Competencies	**32. Planning and decision making**—Child learns beginning skills of how to plan ahead and makes decisions at an appropriate developmental level. **33. Interpersonal competence**—Child interacts with adults and children and can make friends. Child expresses and articulates feelings in appropriate ways and empathizes with others. **34. Cultural competence**—Child has knowledge of and comfort with people of different cultural/racial/ethnic backgrounds. **35. Resistance skills**—Child begins to develop the ability to resist negative peer pressure and dangerous situations. **36. Peaceful conflict resolution**—Child attempts to resolve conflicts nonviolently.
Positive Identity	**37. Personal power**—Child begins to feel he or she has control over "things that happen to me." Child starts to manage frustrations and challenges in ways that have positive results for the child and others. **38. Self-esteem**—Child reports having high self-esteem. **39. Sense of purpose**—Child reports that "my life has a purpose" and actively engages her or his skills. **40. Positive view of personal future**—Child is hopeful and positive about her or his personal future.

40 Developmental Assets for Youth

MIDDLE & HIGH SCHOOL–AGES TWELVE TO EIGHTEEN

SEARCH INSTITUTE *has identified the following building blocks of healthy development that help young people grow up healthy, caring, and responsible. SEARCH INSTITUTE has surveyed almost one hundred thousand sixth- to twelfth-graders in 213 cities and towns across the country to measure their asset levels.*

ASSET TYPE	ASSET NAME AND DEFINITION
Support	1. **Family support**—Family life provides high levels of love and support.
	2. **Positive family communication**—Young person and her or his parent(s) communicate positively, and young person is willing to seek parental advice and counsel.
	3. **Other adult relationships**—Young person receives support from three or more nonparent adults.
	4. **Caring neighborhood**—Young person experiences caring neighbors.
	5. **Caring school climate**—School provides a caring, encouraging environment.
	6. **Parent involvement in schooling**—Parent(s) are actively involved in helping young person succeed in school.
Empowerment	7. **Community values youth**—Young person perceives that adults in the community value youth.
	8. **Youth as resources**—Young people are given useful roles in the community.
	9. **Service to others**—Young person serves in the community one hour or more per week.
	10. **Safety**—Young person feels safe at home, school, and in the neighborhood.
Boundaries & Expectations	11. **Family boundaries**—Family has clear rules and consequences, and monitors the young person's whereabouts.
	12. **School boundaries**—School provides clear rules and consequences.
	13. **Neighborhood boundaries**—Neighbors take responsibility for monitoring young people's behavior.
	14. **Adult role models**—Parent(s) and other adults model positive, responsible behavior.
	15. **Positive peer influence**—Young person's best friends model responsible behavior.
	16. **High expectations**—Both parent(s) and teachers encourage the young person to do well.
Constructive Use of Time	17. **Creative activities**—Young person spends three or more hours per week in lessons or practice in music, theater, or other arts.
	18. **Youth programs**—Young person spends three or more hours per week in sports, clubs, or organizations at school and/or in community organizations.
	19. **Religious community**—Young person spends one or more hours per week in activities in a religious institution.
	20. **Time at home**—Young person is out with friends "with nothing special to do" two or fewer nights per week.

ASSET TYPE	ASSET NAME AND DEFINITION
Commitment to Learning	**21. Achievement motivation**—Young person is motivated to do well in school.
	22. School engagement—Young person is actively engaged in learning.
	23. Homework—Young person reports doing at least one hour of homework every school day.
	24. Bonding to school—Young person cares about her or his school.
	25. Reading for pleasure—Young person reads for pleasure three or more hours per week.
Positive Values	**26. Caring**—Young person places high value on helping other people.
	27. Equality and social justice—Young person places high value on promoting equality and reducing hunger and poverty.
	28. Integrity—Young person acts on convictions and stands up for her or his beliefs.
	29. Honesty—Young person "tells the truth even when it is not easy."
	30. Responsibility—Young person accepts and takes personal responsibility.
	31. Restraint—Young person believes it is important not to be sexually active or to use alcohol or other drugs.
Social Competencies	**32. Planning and decision making**—Young person knows how to plan ahead and make choices.
	33. Interpersonal competence—Young person has empathy, sensitivity, and friendship skills.
	34. Cultural competence—Young person has knowledge of and comfort with people of different cultural/racial/ethnic backgrounds.
	35. Resistance skills—Young person can resist negative peer pressure and dangerous situations.
	36. Peaceful conflict resolution—Young person seeks to resolve conflict nonviolently.
Positive Identity	**37. Personal power**—Young person feels he or she has control over "things that happen to me."
	38. Self-esteem—Young person reports having a high self-esteem.
	39. Sense of purpose—Young person reports that "my life has a purpose."
	40. Positive view of personal future—Young person is optimistic about her or his personal future.

Asset-Building Ideas for All Adults

All adults have the ability and responsibility to build assets in children and youth. Young people benefit greatly when they have involved, caring adults in their lives. You don't need to invest a lot of time and energy to start building assets. You can start small and easy.

Some ideas to get started:

☐ Learn more about asset building. Attend an asset-building training. Read materials on asset building. Surround yourself with asset building materials, such as posting the list of forty developmental assets.

☐ Learn the names of children and teenagers who live near you or who work in shops or community centers you frequent. Greet them by name.

☐ Model a positive, healthy lifestyle. Control and resolve anger issues in your life. Practice peaceful conflict resolution (asset #36). Be motivated to achieve (asset #21). Advocate and work for equality and social justice (asset #27).

☐ Support local efforts to provide safe spaces for young people to meet and congregate.

☐ Expect young people to behave responsibly. When they do not, tell them what you expect and how you would like them to act.

☐ Take time to play or talk with young people who live near you or work with you.

☐ Look at the list of forty developmental assets at least once a week and commit to at least one act of asset building every day.

☐ Support initiatives designed to expand opportunities for children and youth to participate in teams, clubs, and organizations.

☐ Build at least one sustained, caring relationship with a child or adolescent.

☐ Examine your attitudes about children and youth. See young people as resources rather than as problems.

☐ Thank people who work with children and youth, such as teachers, youth group leaders, social service providers, and clergy.

☐ Organize a "gently used" musical instrument drive to encourage people to donate musical instruments for young people who are not able to purchase their own.

☐ Look out for the children around you. Help keep them safe. Report dangerous and inappropriate behaviors to parents, school administrators, or law enforcement officials.

☐ Get involved in an organized volunteer effort with children and youth. You can find these through local schools, youth-serving organizations, congregations, parks and recreation, and other community-based organizations.

☐ Take time to nurture your own assets by spending time with supportive people, using your time constructively, and reflecting on your own values.

Asset-Building Ideas for Parents

The underlying shift for becoming an asset-building parent is to become proactive and engaged. It entails focusing your attention, energy, and resources on the things your children need to grow up healthy.

Here are a few ideas to get started in building assets:

☐ Post the list of forty developmental assets on your refrigerator door. Each day purposefully nurture at least one asset in each family member.

☐ Model—and talk about—the values and priorities you wish to pass on to your children.

☐ Limit television watching. Find other interesting and meaningful activities for children to do—some with you, some with their friends, some by themselves.

☐ Stay in contact with teachers about your children's progress rather than waiting for report cards.

☐ Think of your children and teenagers as "practicing" adults. Teach them something practical, such as how to change a tire on the car, how to sort the laundry, or how to create a monthly budget.

☐ Regularly do things with your child, including projects around the house, recreational activities, and service projects. Let your children or teenagers choose which activities to do together as a family from time to time.

☐ Talk to your children about assets. Ask them for suggestions of ways to strengthen assets.

☐ Introduce your children to other neighborhood adults, and help them get acquainted.

☐ Take time to nurture your own assets. Spend time with supportive people. Use your time constructively. Reflect on your own values and commitments.

☐ Eat at least one meal together every day.

☐ Become active in your child's education through school activities, monitoring homework, and having conversations about school and learning.

☐ Negotiate boundaries and consequences for the whole family.

☐ Develop a family mission statement that focuses on building assets. Then use it as a guide for family decisions and priorities.

☐ Choose a service project to do together, such as collecting cans for a food drive.

☐ Be a friend and asset builder for the friends of your children. Welcome them into your home.

Asset-Building Ideas for Children

No one is too young to build assets. Many children have a lot of ideas on how to build assets in new ways.

Here are ideas on how to get started as an asset builder:

☐ Say hi to people you know. Smile at them.

☐ Help others who need help. Be nice to other children and adults.

☐ Follow the rules that adults set. If you don't understand a rule, ask questions.

☐ Talk to an adult about your day. Do you have time to do all these things: learn? play? relax? be with your family? be with other children? Do you like how you spend time each day? Why or why not?

☐ Play with a younger child. Play what the child wants to play.

☐ Learn more about something you're curious about. Look at books. Ask adults about the subject. Find out if there are any projects you can do to learn more.

☐ Thank people when they do something nice for you.

☐ Be honest about your feelings. Use words to describe your feelings.

☐ Teach others skills you know but they don't. Can you stand on your head? whistle? tie shoes? do yo-yo stunts? make up jokes?

☐ Invite someone new to play with your friends.

☐ Look at books with another child. Read aloud if you know how, or tell a story by looking at the pictures.

☐ Go easy on yourself when you make mistakes. Mistakes aren't bad, and everyone makes mistakes. In fact, mistakes help you learn.

☐ Notice how others are acting around you. Does someone seem sad? happy? scared? Ask the person about how he or she is feeling.

☐ Volunteer to help someone do a chore or a task.

☐ Try new, safe activities—even if you're not sure you'll like them. Take a risk to do something new, then congratulate yourself after you've done so.

☐ When someone does something that hurts your feelings, tell that person. Explain why what was said hurt you.

☐ Give your family ideas on how to have more fun together.

☐ Do what you like to do. Practice and challenge yourself to learn more.

☐ Find out more about assets. Start building assets today.

Asset-Building Ideas for Youth

You can make a difference by building assets. Some teenagers have started by learning the names of more of their peers at school. Some have built assets by building relationships with younger children. Others have focused their efforts on making a difference in their school, congregation, or community.

Here are ideas on how to get started as an asset builder:

☐ Learn the names of your neighbors, including adults, children, and other teenagers. Ask one of your parents to introduce you to neighbors you don't know.

☐ Post the forty developmental assets in your room or in your locker. Choose a different asset each day and focus on building it in your friends.

☐ Sample a variety of experiences and activities in music, theater, art, and athletics, not only in your school but also in your community. Try not to specialize too early.

☐ Participate in at least one group, team, or sport; or find something creative that appeals to you, such as acting or making crafts.

☐ Get to know an adult you admire.

☐ Replace put-downs with affirmations. Make sure your teasing is supportive, not harsh.

☐ Become a walking dictionary and encyclopedia about asset building. Learn more about the research and the implications of the asset framework.

☐ Write a note to or call one of the main asset builders in your life. Thank her or him for making a difference in your life.

☐ Think of your best friends. Do they build you up or drag you down? How do they build assets in you? How do you build assets in them?

☐ Go out of your way to greet the neighbors that you know.

☐ Start a book club with friends and read just for fun.

☐ Focus on developing your resistance skills more (asset #35).

☐ Talk about the forty developmental assets with members of your family. Which assets do family members think are the strongest in your family?

☐ If you have a part-time job during the school year, limit your work schedule to fifteen or fewer hours per week to allow time for schoolwork and other activities that are important to your overall development.

☐ Identify something each family member is good at and focus on that. If your mom is great at geography, turn to her when you're reading a map or needing help with a geography assignment. If your dad is a whiz at math, seek him out for making a savings plan or for assistance with a math problem.

☐ Talk with young people in your neighborhood about what's good about where you live. Also discuss how the neighborhood could change for the better. Work together in making some simple, positive changes.

☐ Even if your family provides a warm, caring, supportive place to grow, also seek support through adults in schools, community organizations, and congregations.

☐ Examine the cocurricular activities you are in. Are you feeling challenged? Do you enjoy the activities? Do you feel you have enough time to do the activities, complete homework, and also have time for yourself, family, and friends? If not, consider making some changes.

☐ Seek out adult mentors and healthy role models.

☐ Become involved in a social issue that interests you, such as poverty, civil rights, hunger, child abuse and neglect, or discrimination.

☐ Get involved in the community doing volunteer community service. Look for other service opportunities.

☐ Choose one way to build a relationship with a child, perhaps by baby-sitting, playing catch with a child in the neighborhood, or volunteering as a coaching assistant.

☐ Gather information about your future goals and dreams. Seek out people who can help make your dreams come true.

Integrating Asset Building

INTO WORSHIP

In most congregations young people are expected to participate in worship alongside adults. Indeed, worship services are the most consistent and visible times when the intergenerational community of faith gathers. These experiences can connect young people with the resources of their faith tradition, offering a sense of purpose, hope, and direction. In addition, worship services offer an opportunity to build community across generations, while also calling the community to action for children and youth. Here are a few specific ideas for integrating asset building into worship. Adapt and use them to fit within your faith tradition.

☐ Ask children and youth what they like and don't like about the worship service. Get their ideas for making it more interesting, meaningful, and relevant.

☐ Have a sermon series on asset building that ties it to the congregation's faith tradition and beliefs.

☐ Involve youth on a worship planning team.

☐ Involve young people as readers, lay liturgists, or other roles in worship appropriate for your faith tradition. In some traditions, it is also appropriate for young people to provide leadership for an entire worship service.

☐ Assign young people a regular responsibility in worship. This might include having them be responsible for collecting offering every week. Or a children's choir might be responsible for regularly providing music.

☐ Create and include inserts on asset building in the bulletins for several weeks.

☐ Ask young people to create banners or other visual aids to enhance the worship service.

☐ Ask young people to provide leadership through puppetry, clowning, drama, mime, liturgical dance, and other art forms appropriate to your faith tradition.

☐ Include at least one hymn in each service that is familiar to children and youth.

☐ Regularly feature children and youth choirs.

☐ Tie worship themes to youth and children's ministry activities such as service projects, and special trips.

☐ Evaluate the language and symbols in worship to discover whether they are meaningful to young people. To enhance communication, either adapt the worship or educate youth so they can participate more fully.

☐ Always include stories and examples relevant to young people in sermons and liturgies. Celebrate their successes, address their struggles and questions, and connect the faith tradition with their world.

☐ Include an "asset-building minute" during announcements or at other times during the service. Invite people to tell what they are doing to build assets, or give tips for how members of the congregation can build assets.

☐ Sponsor a children's Sabbath or a similar service focused on children.

Integrating Asset Building
INTO FELLOWSHIP ACTIVITIES

In addition to providing care in times of crisis, most congregations often have community-building, fellowship, or social activities. These may include refreshments after a worship service, midweek dinners, dances, and picnics. Some ways to make these activities have an asset-building emphasis include:

☐ Involve young people in planning and/or leading congregation-wide social activities.

☐ When providing refreshments, be sure they are appropriate for children. For example, serve juice as well as coffee.

☐ Plan games at picnics and other events that are appropriate for all ages, not just for children or for those who are physically fit.

☐ If an activity requires entertainment, ask young people to lead it.

☐ Have mixers that intentionally help generations mingle and get to know each other.

☐ Create clear boundaries and expectations of how you want children, youth, and adults to act in your church's social activities. Promote these boundaries and expectations, and give people support in enforcing them.

☐ For congregational meals create simple place mats with "talk trigger" questions written on them to help people get to know each other better.

☐ Develop new fellowship activities that are geared toward families, such as celebrating National Family Week. Many churches honor this week in November.

☐ Include children and youth in the cleanup. Young children can pick up and throw away used cups. Teenagers can wash down tabletops. Adults can work side by side with young people and wash dishes.

☐ Emphasize creative activities (asset #17) in some of your fellowship activities. Sponsor an all-church art festival for a month in which children, teenagers, and adults are given space to display their artwork. Invite everyone to your church's "gallery" opening.

Integrating Asset Building

INTO CONGREGATIONAL CARE

Most congregations have a strong emphasis on providing care and support for members, particularly in times of crisis. This care may be expressed by lay caregivers (deacons, elders, lay leaders) or by clergy through counseling or pastoral care. Often the people who provide this care think of their roles as primarily caring for adults. If a young person needs help or support, a youth worker is deployed for the job.

While it is certainly important for those who work directly with young people to provide support and care, it is also important that the congregation integrate young people into these systems of support. It becomes an important bridge to the larger community of faith, signaling to the young that the whole community cares for them and values them. Here are some steps to take:

☐ Train young people to be caregivers to others, children and adults as well as other youth.

☐ If the congregation assigns caregivers to families, be sure they provide support to all members of families—including children and youth—not just adults.

☐ When caregivers visit homes, take time to talk with children and youth.

☐ Help caregivers remember and celebrate milestones in young people's lives, such as birthdays, learning to drive, end of school year, and special holidays.

☐ Consider matching a caring adult with each child and teenager in your congregation. As new members join, continue finding an adult member who can be their assigned caregiver. Also consider having senior high youth and young adults be caregivers of younger children and younger teenagers.

☐ Set up prayer chains that are accessible for children and youth in addition to adults. Also include children and youth in praying for other members of your congregation.

☐ Start a peer-helping program. For example, offer a support group to help young people who are newcomers to adjust to your congregation.

☐ Encourage everyone to be a caregiver for children and youth, even those who aren't in your church's care program. Everyone can learn the names of young people around them and create a climate of caring by greeting them by name.

☐ Send notes or make a phone call to people whom you're praying for so they know that someone is thinking and praying for them. Children and youth can make these cards and phone calls, too.

☐ Educate clergy, mentors, and others who provide counseling about asset building so they can integrate the framework into their roles.

Integrating Asset Building

INTO FACILITIES MAINTENANCE AND OPERATIONS

At first glance it might seem like the operational functions of a congregation's facility have little to do with asset building. But they can and do. Sometimes you only see the relationship when something goes wrong: The janitor gets upset that the youth room is messy. The congregation's board resists a plan to invite neighborhood youth to programs or activities in the building because "they might mess things up." Here are some steps to take:

☐ Design some facilities maintenance or building tasks as service projects for children and youth.

☐ On a regular basis, make facilities available for a youth "hangout" or a homework room.

☐ Set and communicate clear policies about how everyone in the congregation is expected to treat the facilities—and the consequences for not respecting those policies.

☐ Evaluate facilities to ensure they are accessible to children. For example, can younger children reach the water fountains?

☐ If you use volunteers to do cleanup after events or activities, include children and youth.

☐ Find ways for people who maintain your facility to have some interaction with members of your congregation. Too often janitors and facility managers work during the off hours and they don't get to know the children and youth, and young people don't get to know them.

☐ Have young people set up a meeting with your janitor to find out what they can do to make the janitor's job easier.

☐ Encourage your janitor to link up with other janitors from other churches to talk about creative solutions to problems and how to make the church facility a place that builds assets.

☐ With young people, notice what's working. Encourage young people to leave thank you notes on chalkboards or to send notes to the janitor, thanking her or him for work well-done.

Asset-Building Songs and Hymns

Music is an integral part of worship, youth group activities, children's education, and children's ministry. Music moves us, teaches us, and inspires us. Here is a sampling of asset-building songs and hymns.

Support Assets	• "How Happy Is Each Child of God," lyrics by Dwyn M. Mounger, song from Este's *Psalmes*. • "Jesu, Jesu, Fill Us with Your Love," a Ghanaian folk melody translated and adapted by Tom Colvin, arranged by Jane Marshall. • "Blest Be the Tie That Binds," lyrics by John Fawcett, composed by Johann Georg Nägeli, arranged by Lowell Mason. • "Jesus Loves Me!" lyrics by Anna Barlett Warner, composed by William Batchelder Bradbury. • "Though I May Speak," lyrics by Hal Hopson, an English folk melody, harmonized by John Weaver.
Empowerment Assets	• "All Things Bright and Beautiful," lyrics by Cecil Frances Alexander, an English melody adapted by Martin Shaw. • "Child of Blessing, Child of Promise," lyrics by Ronald Cole-Turner, composed by V. Earle Copes. • "Called as Partners in Christ's Service," lyrics by Jane Parker Huber. • "Savior, Like a Shepherd Lead Us," lyrics from Thrupp's *Hymns for the Young*, composed by William Batchelder Bradbury. • "We Give Thee but Thine Own," lyrics by William Walsham How, composition from Mason and Webb's *Cantica Laudis*. (See verses 3 and 4.)
Boundaries & Expectations Assets	• "With Grateful Hearts Our Faith Professing," lyrics by Fred Kaan, composed by Clement Cottewill Scholefield. • "Dearest Jesus, We Are Here," lyrics by Benjamin Schmolck and translated by Catherine Winkworth, composed by Johann Rudolph Ahle, harmonized by Johann Sebastian Bach. • "O Lord of Every Shining Constellation," lyrics by Albert F. Bayly, composed by V. Earle Copes. • "We Gather Together," lyrics translated by Theodore Baker from a Dutch hymn, harmonized by Edward Kremser from a Dutch folk song. • "We Gather Here to Bid Farewell," lyrics by Margaret Clarkson, composition from *Musikalisches Handbuch*, harmonized by William Henry Monk. • "We Are Your People," lyrics by Brian Wren, composed by John W. Wilson. (See verses 4 and 5.)
Constructive-Use-of-Time Assets	• "I Danced in the Morning," lyrics by Sydney Carter, an American Shaker melody harmonized by Sydney Carter. • "He Keeps Me Singing," lyrics and composition by Luther B. Bridgers. • "Come, Thou Almighty King," lyrics from the *Collection of Hymns for Social Worship*, composed by Felice de Giardini. • "Amazing Grace, How Sweet the Sound," lyrics by John Newton, composition from *Virginia Harmony*, arranged by Edwin O. Excell. • "God of the Ages, Whose Almighty Hand," lyrics by Daniel Crane Roberts, composed by George William Warren. • "All Glory, Laud, and Honor," lyrics by Theodulph of Orleans, translated by John Mason Neale, composed by Melchior Teschner, arranged by William Henry Monk. • "Jesus Christ Is Risen Today," lyrics and composition from *Lyra Davidica*. Verse 4 lyrics by Charles Wesley. (See verses 2 and 4.)

ASSET-BUILDING SONGS AND HYMNS

Commitment-to-Learning Assets	• "Seek Ye First," lyrics and composition by Karen Lafferty. • "God of Grace and God of Glory," lyrics by Harry Emerson Fosdick, composition by John Hughes. • "Open My Eyes That I May See," lyrics and composition by Clara H. Scott. • "Take My Life," lyrics by Frances Ridley Havergal, composition by H.A. César Malan. (See verse 4.) • "Savior, Teach Me Day by Day," lyrics by Jane E. Leeson, composition from the Innocents, *Parish Choir.* • "Earth and All Stars," lyrics by Herbert Frederick Brokering, composition by David N. Johnson. (See verses 3 and 4.) • "O Master, Let Me Walk with Thee," lyrics by Washington Gladden, composition by Henry Percy Smith.
Positive-Values Assets	• "O for a World," lyrics by Miriam Therese Winter, composition by Carl Gotthelf Gläser, arranged by Lowell Mason. • "This Is My Father's World," lyrics by Maltbie Davenport Babcock, composition by Franklin L. Sheppard. • "God, You Spin the Whirling Planets," lyrics by Jane Parker Huber, composition by Franz Joseph Haydn. • "God of the Sparrow," lyrics by Jaroslav J. Vajda, composition by Carl F. Schalk.
Social-Competencies Assets	• "For the Beauty of the Earth," lyrics by Folliott Sandford Pierpoint, composition by Conrad Kocher. (See verse 4.) • "O God the Creator," lyrics by Elizabeth Haile and Cecil Corbett, composition by Joy F. Patterson. • "Help Us Accept Each Other," lyrics by Fred Kaan, composition by Doreen Potter. • "Here, O Lord, Your Servants Gather," lyrics by Tokuo Yamaguchi, translated by Everett M. Stowe, composition by Isao Koizumi. • "In Christ There Is No East or West," lyrics by John Oxenham, composition by Alexander Robert Reinagle. • "When Israel Was in Egypt's Land," an African-American spiritual, arranged by Melva W. Costen. • "I've Got Peace Like a River," an African-American spiritual.
Positive-Identity Assets	• "Let Us Talents and Tongues Employ," lyrics by Fred Kaan, a Jamaican folk melody adapted by Doreen Potter. • "Lord, When I Came Into This Life," lyrics by Fred Kaan, an American folk melody arranged by Annabel Morris Buchanan. • "Here I Am, Lord," lyrics and composition by Daniel L. Schutte. • "God of Our Life," lyrics by Hugh Thomson Kerr, composition by Charles Henry Purday, harmonized by John Weaver. • "I'm Gonna Live So God Can Use Me," an African-American spiritual arranged by Wendell Whalum. • "Just as I Am, Without One Plea," lyrics by Charlotte Elliott, composition by William Batchelder Bradbury. • "My Hope Is Built on Nothing Less," lyrics by Edward Mote, composition by William Batchelder Bradbury.

Additional Resources

APPENDIX 2

Additional Asset-Building Resources

Search Institute provides a variety of tools and resources to support asset building in many parts of a community. These include materials specifically written for congregations, but also other resources that can be easily applied to congregations. These materials are available from Search Institute, 1-877-240-7251, or www.search-institute.org.

Just for Congregations

Building Assets in Congregations: A Practical Guide for Helping Youth Grow Up Healthy. This book offers a comprehensive guide to creating an asset-building congregation. It's written for youth workers, religious leaders, volunteers, and others who care about young people in congregations. In addition to helpful information on creating a vision and planning, it includes work sheets, handouts, and ten reproducible bulletin inserts for sharing information about the assets.

Get on Board! Presentations and Activities for Introducing Asset Building in Congregations. This set of short presentations is designed to introduce congregations to asset building. It includes overhead and handout masters and is ideal for raising awareness in individual congregations.

Integrating Assets Into Congregations: A Curriculum for Trainers. This complete training kit offers training designs for eighteen hours of training for teams. It covers the implications of developmental assets for all areas of congregational life. Designed for experienced trainers.

Kids Have a Lot to Give: How Congregations Can Nurture the Habits of Giving and Serving for the Common Good. This guide challenges congregations with a systematic examination of how to help young people develop lifelong habits of service to others and financial giv-

ing. It offers practical ideas for how congregations can become communities that nurture generous and compassionate young people.

Networking Congregations for Asset Building: A Tool Kit. This collection of ideas, information activities, and practical tools is designed to help congregations of many faith traditions work together to build assets for their own young people and those in the wider community.

A Foundation for Success: Video and Discussion Guide. Designed to show asset building in action, this twenty-five-minute video offers ideas and examples from many faith traditions on how asset building can be integrated into the activities and life of a religious institution.

Youth Development in Congregations: An Exploration of the Potential and Barriers. This report examines congregational youth work in the United States and the potential for a focus on asset-building congregations. It includes data from a survey on the attitudes and needs of religious youth workers.

Tapping the Potential: Discovering Congregations' Role in Building Assets in Youth. This short brochure introduces the potential for asset building in congregations. It is particularly valuable in introducing the idea of asset building to religious leaders.

In-Depth Information

All Kids Are Our Kids: What Communities Must Do to Raise Caring and Responsible Children and Adolescents. Written by the original creator of the asset framework, Search Institute president Peter L. Benson, this book explains the asset framework and its background. It also presents the vision of asset-building communities and basic strategies to help people and institutions recognize the role they play in raising healthy children and youth.

A Fragile Foundation: The State of Developmental Assets Among American Youth. Based on a sample of almost one hundred thousand youth in 213 communities, this report looks at youth today through the developmental asset lens. With easy-to-read text and charts, the report is a necessary tool for understanding the developmental asset framework. It includes detailed information on the state of assets among various populations of youth.

What Kids Need to Succeed: Proven, Practical Ways to Raise Good Kids. This easy-to-read book features practical and specific information about building assets at home, in the congregation, at school, and in the community. With more than nine hundred common-sense ideas (including hundreds specifically for congregations), it is the most extensive collection of asset-building ideas available.

Awareness-Raising Tools

40 Assets: Start Over, Starting Now video. This eight-minute video provides a brief overview of the assets using stories and examples from people across the United States. Includes a discussion guide.

150 Ways to Show Kids You Care. This popular handout provides concrete, specific ways adults can build positive relationships with children and youth—one of the first steps in asset building. Also available in Spanish. Sold in packets of twenty.

The Asset Approach/El enfoque en los elementos fundamentales. This eight-page brochure provides an overview of the asset-building approach. It features basic research on assets, a checklist for starting discussions with young people, a list of the assets, and ideas on how anyone can build assets. Available in packets of twenty in English and Spanish.

Pass It On! Ready-to-Use Handouts for Asset Builders. This collection of almost ninety-two photocopiable handouts includes basic asset information and practical ideas to build assets. Several handouts are designed specifically for congregations.

Sharing the Asset Message: 40-Asset Speaker's Kit. This in-depth kit includes a complete script, transparencies, handouts, and stories to use in presenting the assets framework to multiple audiences.

You Can Make a Difference for Kids. This eight-page booklet shows how anyone can and should build developmental assets. It includes

Healthy Communities · Healthy Youth National Conference

Each fall, thousands of asset-building champions and allies gather from across North America to share ideas, be inspired, and learn together. Multiple learning sessions—led by national experts and local practitioners—focus specifically on asset building in congregations.

For more information, visit Search Institute's Web site: www.search-institute.org

tear-out cards with asset lists for children and youth from birth through age eighteen. Sold in packets of twenty.

You Can!: The Asset Categories Poster. This colorful poster highlights the eight categories of developmental assets by giving concrete actions that everyone can take to build assets. Ideal for displaying in halls, entryways, classrooms, and gathering places in congregations and the community.

Asset-Building Tools for Children's and Youth Ministry

An Asset Builder's Guide to Service-Learning. Using a service-learning approach (which emphasizes both action and reflection), this guide shows how asset building can strengthen service efforts. It also addresses intergenerational service and family service.

An Asset Builder's Guide to Youth Leadership. This hands-on guide addresses how to engage young people in meaningful leadership roles within an organization. It offers tools, ideas, tips, and stories that help congregations, schools, and youth organizations build assets by empowering youth to lead.

An Asset Builder's Guide to Youth and Money. Learning to manage money responsibly is an important skill for today's youth. And it's also a great—though often untapped—opportunity to build assets and shape values. It emphasizes responsible use of money, including giving to charity and religious institutions.

Building Assets Together: 135 Group Activities for Helping Youth Succeed. Designed to help young people examine each of the developmental assets, this book includes experiential activities and creative work sheets on each of the forty assets. Use these activities for youth groups, retreats, and religious education.

What Teens Need to Succeed: Proven, Practical Ways to Shape Your Own Future. Written for teenagers, this book is packed with practical ideas, and other information that young people can use to build assets with their friends and in their family, school, congregation, and community. It can be used as a springboard for discussions among youth about how they want to build assets for themselves and others.

What Young Children Need to Succeed: Working Together to Build Assets from Birth to Age Eleven. This book presents hundreds of practical ideas for building assets for infants, toddlers, preschoolers, and elementary-age children. Each chapter includes ideas for how congregations can build assets. An accompanying leader's guide is also available that includes five ready-to-use workshops and reproducible handout masters.

Asset-Building Tools for Working With Families

Parenting with a Purpose: A Positive Approach for Raising Confident, Caring Youth. This sixteen-page booklet shows the roles parents can play in building assets and finding support.

Ideas for Parents: Newsletter Master Set. This collection of fifty two-page newsletter masters (each covering a category of assets or one of the forty assets) is designed for distributing to parents so that they get bite-size pieces of information that help them be more effective and intentional asset builders.

Congregational Wide Activities

Creating Intergenerational Community. This booklet contains seventy-five ideas for bringing adults and youth together, either individually or in groups.

Taking Asset Building Personally: Planning Guide and Personal Action Workbook. This resource kit includes curriculum and personal workbooks for a six-session class on asset building, with a particular focus on what each person, youth or adult, can do to build assets. The planning guide gives ideas for how to set up discussion groups in your organization or community. Ideal for use in adult education, youth groups, or—best of all—intergenerational small groups.

Connecting to the Community

Creating Healthy Communities for Kids video. This twelve-minute video features people from across the United States who are working to unite their communities around asset building. It features stories of how communities are making a positive difference for youth.

Healthy Communities · Healthy Youth Booklet. This booklet introduces the vision of an asset-building community, focusing on the roles that individuals and organizations play in building assets, and basic steps for getting started with a community-wide effort.

Healthy Communities · Healthy Youth Tool Kit. This kit features hundreds of ideas, strategies, and examples for undertaking the practical tasks involved in building a community-wide asset-building initiative. These include planning, budgeting, youth involvement, recruiting volunteers, and many other topics.

Additional Asset-Building Resources

FROM GROUP PUBLISHING

Many of Group's resources support the eight categories of development assets. These books are available from Group Publishing, 1-800-447-1070.

Support Assets

130 Ways to Involve Parents in Youth Ministry. Bring parents and teenagers together with service projects, meetings, and activities.

The Family-Friendly Church by Ben Freudenburg With Rick Lawrence. Discover how certain programming can often short-circuit your church's ability to truly strengthen families—and what you can do about it!

No More Us & Them: 100 Ways to Bring Your Youth & Church Together edited by Amy Simpson. Find lots of ideas for getting young people connected to people of all ages in your church through intergenerational activities and service projects.

Empowerment Assets

Hands-On Service Ideas for Children's Ministry. Help children understand the value of serving others with these hands-on activities designed especially for elementary-age kids.

Hands-On Service Ideas for Youth Groups by Steve Case and Fred Cornforth. Use this collection of over one hundred creative ways to involve your teenagers in service.

Kids Taking Charge: Youth-Led Youth Ministry by Thom and Joani Schultz. This classic book shows how to empower young people to become real leaders in your church.

Boundaries & Expectations Assets

The Discipline Guide for Children's Ministry by Jody Capehart and Gordon and Becki West. With this book, you'll implement classroom management techniques that work and make teaching fun again.

Successful Youth Mentoring. These twenty-four sessions for mentors help adults develop leadership characteristics in young people.

Constructive-Use-of-Time Assets

Creative Can-Do Crafts by Lois Keffer. More than seventy-five all-new craft projects will encourage your kids' self-confidence and build their Christian faith.

The Warm and Wonderful Church Nursery by Kim Sikes and Lori Haynes Niles. Here are pick-and-choose ideas for creating meaningful ways to grab and hold the attention of babies in your nursery.

Strategic Youth Ministry: 30 Keys to Life-Change in Teenagers by Eugene C. Roehlkepartain and others. This book from Search Institute offers a comprehensive, practical approach to youth ministry that keeps kids involved and growing in faith.

Commitment-to-Learning Assets

The Dirt on Learning by Thom and Joani Schultz. This thought-provoking book explores what Jesus' Parable of the Sower says about effective teaching and learning.

Do It! Active Learning in Youth Ministry, Revised and Updated by Thom and Joani Schultz. Discover how to design your own simple, fun programs that actively involve teenagers.

Positive-Values Assets

Character Builders. Lead children through Bible-based activities that help them make Christlike decisions and grow in honesty and nine other character traits.

Character Counts!: 40 Youth Ministry Devotions From Extraordinary Christians by Karl Leuthauser. Inspire your kids with these forty youth ministry devotions from the lives of extraordinary Christians who are authentic heroes.

Social-Competencies Assets

Building Community in Youth Groups by Denny Rydberg. You'll discover over one hundred ready-to-use activities to build community in your group.

Friend-Makers & Crowdbreakers for Children's Ministry. Help children meet each other for the first time, get to know each other, and become real friends.

Positive-Identity Assets

101 Affirmations for Teenagers. Build relationships with teenagers as you encourage them to appreciate who God has made them to be.

Everyone's-a-Winner Games for Children's Ministry. Build kids' confidence and make everyone feel like a winner with more than one hundred team-building games.